"The church would be Christ's new community if everyone in the church loved it like Bob Henderson! In his newest book, Henderson's love is channeled into the determined and creative labor of trying to re-conceive the church for the twenty-first century. Gripped by the love of Jesus Christ for a changing world and generations, Henderson raises just the critical questions for fresh consideration and action that we must all take seriously."

—MARK LABBERTON
President, Fuller Theological Seminary, Pasadena, California

"At the height of the civil rights movement, Robert Henderson turned the church upside-down when he began integrating his Raleigh-Durham congregation. Ever since then, Robert has passionately urged the church to return to its central mission in the world. Inspired by Silicon Valley's early roots, Robert offers a provocative design for the Christian community that's relevant to the emerging generation and enables the church to flourish."

—SHERRI HUTTER
Senior Director, Strategic Initiatives, Salesforce

"With the same wit and humor that characterizes his earlier works, Bob Henderson prompts us to reimagine the church as small, creative, intentionally relational communities . . . Henderson persuasively argues that reclaiming the church for the next generation requires dealing with its institutional baggage yet continuing to proclaim God's love for humanity as his new creation."

—ERIK VINCENT
Director of Global Studies, Holy Innocents High School

"Robert Henderson's *Homebrew Churches* is an incredibly valuable read for everyone who cares about the future of the Church. In it, readers nudged to remember how we were created for community and called to be agents of God's new creation. As someone on the frontline with tomorrow's children, I can assure you Robert gets it! I am both challenged and refreshed by this book."

—**TROY EARNEST**
Area Director, Young Life East Atlanta

Homebrew Churches

Homebrew Churches

Reconceiving the Church
for Tomorrow's Children

Robert Thornton Henderson

WIPF & STOCK · Eugene, Oregon

HOMEBREW CHURCHES
Reconceiving the Church for Tomorrow's Children

Copyright © 2018 Robert Thornton Henderson. All rights reserved. Except for brief quotations in critical publications or reviews, no part of this book may be reproduced in any manner without prior written permission from the publisher. Write: Permissions, Wipf and Stock Publishers, 199 W. 8th Ave., Suite 3, Eugene, OR 97401.

Wipf & Stock
An Imprint of Wipf and Stock Publishers
199 W. 8th Ave., Suite 3
Eugene, OR 97401

www.wipfandstock.com

Scripture quotations are from the Holy Bible, English Standard Version® (ESV®), copyright © 2001 by Crossway, a publishing ministry of Good News Publishers. All rights reserved.

PAPERBACK ISBN: 978-1-5326-4227-2
HARDCOVER ISBN: 978-1-5326-4228-9
EBOOK ISBN: 978-1-5326-4229-6

Manufactured in the U.S.A.   01/15/18

To the late Pete Hammond, whose friendship and continual encouragements
to me over many years have profoundly influenced my life
and my writings.

Contents

Preface
Tomorrow's Children: The Emergence of the *iGens* | ix

Chapter 1
Homebrew Churches: Small, Creative,
and Intentionally Relational | 1

Chapter 2
Reclaiming the Church's Founding Purpose | 12

Chapter 3
The All-Consuming Focus: Christ | 25

Chapter 4
The First Gift: The Teaching Shepherd | 33

Chapter 5
The Gift of Apostle | 48

Chapter 6
The Gift of Prophet | 59

Chapter 7
The Gift of Evangelist | 68

Chapter 8
The Book of Revelation: Living in the Apocalypse | 77

Epilogue | 87

Preface

Tomorrow's Children: The Emergence of the *iGens*

A recent article in the *The Atlantic Monthly* spoke to the now reality that "churchgoing" is a diminishing habit, or factor, in our culture. It is always more convenient to lament the passing of the familiar past then to engage the reasons for the change, or the potential of the present, or especially the portent of what is coming down the road of the future. It is much more convenient to try to impose the patterns and values in which our former generation was formed than to seek to exegete the influences that are determining the emerging generation.

What is unseen, given the fact that we have been undergoing what might be designated as a *cultural diastrophism* within the past century in which the subterranean, out-of-sight cultural tectonic plates have been shifting so that the dominance of the Christendom Era, in which the Christian faith and church held dominance, is no longer a given. There have been those colorful battles such as the famous Scopes Trial in Tennessee, in which a fairly rigid disdain for science, and especially for the theory of evolution, was challenged and defeated in court to the chagrin of a considerable portion of the churchgoing populace. There was the struggle within the church in which what was known as the fundamentalist-modernist controversy divided the church and caused a lot of damage.

There were in place, almost universally in the West, "blue laws" that had to do with the legal requirement of Sabbath-keeping, according to the traditions of Christendom. There were frequent attempts to make the drinking of alcohol illegal (though it never worked), and so came the attempt to legalize prohibition. But those cultural tectonic plates were shifting. People went to church because it was expected of respectable folk and, perhaps more realistically, because there wasn't much else to do, what with the blue laws.

Then came two world wars, especially World War II. Those young men and women who had never known much beyond their own communities were exposed to cultures abroad. As one of the popular songs of World War I put is so colorfully, "How are you going to keep them down on the farm once they've seen Paree?" Yet there had been a certain predictable comfort in the traditions that had been inherited.

World War II exhibited this more studied cultural change that is mirrored in the generations that have emerged since then. Generations have very porous boundaries and are not at all hermetically sealed from one another, but they do exhibit patterns that gifted sociologists[1] have studied and defined for us, and their studies say *worlds* about what we are seeing in demonstration of each generation, and we need to stop and look at those. To say, there are always those who are totally anchored to the past and those who have eyes for the emerging future, and they don't always fit easily into any generational description. We observe this regularly in politics, in religion, in education, in ethnicity, and in a plethora of cultural realities.

In this book, it is my desire, at least, to propose that the creativity of the emerging generation (tomorrow's children) raises multiple causes for hope and anticipation for the church, and

1. Sociologist Neal Howe and Strauss and William Howe have been at the forefront of these studies, but have been joined with many offering helpful understanding of what we are observing in each succeeding generation.

for the new global community now so accessible, what with the exponential potential made available because the information and communication resources of the Internet—along with the accompanying cultural liabilities. Forms, patterns, and traditions from the past may or may not be of value, and part of the task in exegeting the culture is to continually be discerning what are the treasures that need to be preserved, but also to know when past patterns are being displaced by creative new forms and realities. The church cannot escape this dynamic.

But for the moment, as we begin, it is worthwhile to take a pause and look at the various generational cultures and to discern what was forming them, knowing that any such appraisal of these cultures is a bit of a caricature, or a sweeping generalization, so that they describe only general colors and patterns, but they will give us some understanding of each. That is critical if we are to understand the emerging generational culture. (And if our reader is one of this emerging generation, our apologies if we misrepresent you.)

The Greatest Generation
(Born between 1900 and 1924)

This generation is so named by Tom Brokaw, and consists of those who came of age in World War II. They had survived the Great Depression with their parents, and were thoroughgoing *traditionalists*. When they had successfully concluded World War II, they wanted to get on with life, and regain the stability they had known before the war. Many were recipients of the G.I. Bill and entered college with energy and determination (I [Bob] should know . . . they were my college contemporaries though I was just a bit too young to be classified with their generation.) That generation is now rapidly disappearing due to aging and death.

Tomorrow's Children: The Emergence of the iGens

The Silent Generation (Born 1925-1945)

This is my generation and it is essentially well named, and because of the Great Depression and World War II it shares many of the traditionalist characteristics of its predecessor generation, though it came of age just at the conclusion of World War II.

The Boomer (or Baby Boom) Generation (Born 1946-1964)

This generation was the result of veterans eager to establish families and return to life as normal, what with all its traditional values. It deserves special attention for our reflection here because, in many ways, it is the dominant culture in the ecclesiastical and political structures of the present with which we deal, and is resistant to the cultural changes irresistibly upon us in this *liminal* time of cultural transition. This is the generation that often sought to escape the traditions and disciplines of their parents. They became the protesting youth culture of the 1960s and early 1970s. They were free spirits and tainted with rebelliousness. They produced the Woodstock Music Festival, which was a monumental capstone of their quest for freedom. They protested the Vietnam War. They were primary agents in the emergence of the civil rights movement (especially in the Black community). . . . But then, disillusioned by so much, they began to revert back into a very traditional and conservative (often politically Republican) philosophy that was (and is) resistant to change and intent on preserving the institutions of the rapidly disappearing culture of their parents. This is now the dominant older generation on our scene, who have a very difficult time appreciating the emerging generation.

Several of those who were to become huge change agents, and the creative minds who would usher in the information/personal computer era, were born late in this generation and essentially bridge into the next: Bill Gates, Steve Jobs, and Tim Cook come to mind.

Tomorrow's Children: The Emergence of the iGens

Generation X (Early 1960s to Late 1970s)

This is, or was, a disillusioned generation, prone to cynicism. It has been called "America's neglected child." It produced (as a significant voice) the grunge musician Kurt Cobain and his band, Nirvana. Cobain's influence on his generation was voiced in his music, and his suicide was a trauma that shook the scene for whom he was a major voice. It is an individualistic, negative, apathetic, independent (frequently drug-dependent) generation . . . but it was the first generation deeply tuned in to the advances in information technology. (Sergei Brin and Larry Page, founders of Google, Jeff Bezos of Amazon, and Tim Cook of Apple were all born early in this period.) It is in this period, also, that there emerged a small group of creative and seminal computer scientists known as the "homebrew computer club," whose appellation we have hijacked for the title of this book. It was a generation uncommitted to its employers, often angry and troubled, while at the same time producing outstanding actors, TV programs, etc. But *GenXers* were something of a fractured generation, so that their successor generation was a huge surprise. (Remember, we're generalizing unapologetically here.)

The Millennial Generation (Early 1980s to Mid-1990s)

Here emerges an optimistic generation whose response to the malaise and problems it had inherited was, "We can fix it!" They had almost no attachment to the traditions of the past and its institutions. (The church and its institutions were becoming a much less significant factor in the culture.) Yet this generation had imagination and creativity, and out of them emerged those huge cultural transformers, such as Sergi Brin and Larry Page, who, as two bored graduate students at Stanford, created the search engine Google. It is within these years that there emerged onto the public stage those persons whose creativity influences all of our lives daily (as mentioned above): Steve Jobst, Mark Zuckerberg, Tim Cook, Jeff

Bazos, and that whole new genre of creative and entrepreneurial geniuses. These guys saw in information technology that potential that their parents and grandparents could not have even remotely imagined. They became billionaires while in their early twenties. They weren't captive to traditions. They created a world of their own.

A biographer of Brin and Page summarizes their attitude with the colorful statement that, for them, if you're going to make tomorrow a better world, then "you've got to break a lot of rules and piss a lot of people off." This is the generation that is the dominant force in so much of the present scene, and pretty much operated totally apart from the traditionalist structures of their Boomer grandparents. They have a global vision of their own.

iGen (Sometimes Referred to as GenZ) (Born after mid-1990s)

The iGen is the generation that can't imagine life without their iPhones. This is a (primarily but not exclusively) younger generation, just emerging into adulthood. It is unique in that it includes from outside its ranks those innovative digital natives from previous generations, though it is primarily that younger generation currently emerging into adulthood. Literally, this is our "tomorrow's children" to which this book is addressed. They are inheriting all the promises and liabilities of the information age, of globalization, of huge movements of immigration, of creating whole new vistas of artificial intelligence, digital connectedness, robotics, patterns of life . . . along with an incredible lack of historical perspective—their world is present and future, and not one formed by yesterday's children. It is these who are our focus.

Yet the cultural context here is no longer dominated by the traditional institutions and expectations of their grandparents. The dominance of Christendom is no longer a significant factor. The caricatures, and often grotesque identification of the Christian faith with political extremists, with all kinds of ethnic prejudices, and with insensitivity to human diversity and needs, have made it quite common to summarily dismiss the Christian faith as an option. The culture is more dominated by something akin to a self-sufficient humanism. That is the dominant culture that has caused something of the reported exodus from traditional church institutions, and caused the media to assume that these iGen folk have no interest in the Christian faith. What is not reported is that Christian high school clubs such as Young Life and collegiate chapters of such ministries as InterVarsity Christian Fellowship are thriving and growing.[2] These adolescent years are a period of healthy questioning and of creativity. There is obviously some kind of built-in need for the components of meaning, authentic relationships, and hope that such organizations are fulfilling.

The problem seems to point to the reality that after the nurturing and authentic relationships experienced in such high school and college fellowships, too many traditional church institutions do not fulfill this need.

It has been said that all humankind share the need for: a *center*, an *authority*, a *creative source*, a *guiding line*, and a *final goal*. The Christian communities that speak clearly to these needs are healthy and contagious. Jesus and the apostolic writers speak directly to that reality. What needs to be explored, and our task here, is to seek to understand what are the dynamics, what are the forms, what are the disciplines and realities that explain and also create such Christian communities? It to be aware that there are many world religions, and in this global culture they are on our doorstep also making claim to provide answers.

Self-sufficient humanism, so pervasive, makes it more common to engage in the lifestyle of the masses, and to sweep those ultimate questions into the closet for some later consideration. The two of us want to pull those questions out into full sunlight and attempt to put together a helpful and encouraging guide for a fresh understanding of the communities of God's New Humanity. Take a walk with us. It is our purpose to provide something of a helpful guidebook for the emerging generation in the midst of all kinds

---

2. Along with other Christian ministries focused on the emerging culture.

of incomparable new discoveries, cultural patterns, and challenges that will be the context of their lives.

Our Moment in the History of the Church

In a very real sense, the church has always been inventing and reinventing itself as it moved out into the wider world. It has always been creating and recreating, innovating and experimenting, conceiving and re-conceiving itself from the very inception, as it has moved into new challenges, different cultures, and changing contexts. To be sure, the church has often gotten sidetracked, distracted, or has become forgetful of its *raison d'etre* along the way. There is wide consensus that it has been subverted from its calling by its obsession with its institutional expressions, i.e., its buildings, ecclesiastical hierarchies, and its dependence on professional clergy. It is fitting for us, then, with the emergence of a dominant *digital world*, and the generation that world is forming, to take a step back, take a deep breath, and take a fresh look at both this culture and the generation it is producing. The iGen culture is one that can be quite dismissive and indifferent toward the church, and essentially ignorant of traditional church institutions and their place in history.

What, then, might the church look like that would be engaging and fruitful among such? The church has always had the prophetic challenge to incarnate the word of God by "rooting up, pulling down, and destroying" the aberrations in God's community that existed, and then "building and planting" that which is faithful to his calling (Jeremiah 1:10).

Yes, there are those moments in history when what might be called *diastrophic* cultural change is making obsolete so many traditional landmarks and launching us into an unknown future. That includes generational patterns of the past, which are displaced, and a generation whose character is being formed as they confront inexplicable new challenges. It is my estimate that we are now at such a moment. It is also my conviction, at the same time, that we must express our huge appreciation for all the faith and faithfulness of those people of God who have gone before us, and whose legacy has been formative in so many of our lives . . . those mystics and missioners, those martyrs and those humanitarians, those theologians and pioneers of church planting in such a huge array of circumstances globally.

And for myself, I am of the Reformed tradition of Christendom, whose moniker is derived from its motto (translated from the Latin): "The church reformed and ever being reformed according to the word of God." It is with that motto, and with all those components in mind, then, that what follows is an attempt to assist my readers in being faithful in this, our own moment in history, provocative and positive in intent.

Chapter 1

Homebrew Churches: Small, Creative, and Intentionally Relational

First off, I need to explain and to unpack the metaphor I have appropriated for my title: *Homebrew Churches*. I need to satisfy the curiosity of my readers about this, and then spell out all the specific potential which it holds.

It may seem strange (even weird) to begin this journey into *Reconceiving the Church for Tomorrow's Children* with this example from the dawning of the personal computer era . . . but in 1975 there were six technically minded electronics enthusiasts who, from various posts, discerned the huge potential that was held in an early microcomputer. Their mutual curiosity ultimately brought these six together, at first casually, then biweekly, in the garage of one of them in Menlo Park, California, for a period of about a year and a half . . . to wonder, to exchange ideas, to test theories, and ultimately to be significantly responsible for the whole cultural impact of the personal computer, which in turn has transformed the way we live today. This group became known as the "Homebrew Computer Club."

It is necessary to observe that at the beginning those six guys had a common vision and dream that called them together, and bonded them to one another. Those six would meet in the evenings of those biweekly meetings, work informally for a few hours, and then frequently retire to some nearby location to socialize over drinks, and to continue to dream together. Out of that small, informal, highly motivated group emerged, ultimately, much that would form the microcomputer industry that we know today. When they had accomplished that which they felt were their goals, they disbanded, though they continued to meet informally thereafter. The influence of the Homebrew Computer Club was huge.

Note, secondly, that they did not assume the permanence of their group, or idolize the group as such, but were basically a set of companions who were goal oriented, focused on encouraging each other in pursuit of a common mission. When that was accomplished, they disbanded, though they remained in close communication with each other out of the friendships forged during those months.

Now, you may be asking, "What does any of this have to do with reconceiving the church?" That is precisely what we need to ask. First, it was composed of acquaintances who were captivated by an idea that was just beyond the horizons of their experience. They were those who were immersed in the daily existential realities of their lives, on the boundaries of this potential. They were eager to process and refine their thinking and insights by the opinion, critique, and interaction with each other. And, ultimately, they were to share what they had mutually discovered into the formation of the Information Age—a truly culture-transforming phenomenon out of this group of six. It will be worthwhile to do an overlay of this Homebrew Computer Club with this quest to achieve a *reconceived church*. It will also compel us to look back at the apostolic teachings, and at the model we have in Jesus Christ, and so with all the similarities that emerge . . . and then to look beyond what were the patterns that have dominated the passing era.

The previous era that formed yesterday's children is commonly designated as the *Christendom era*, and as that which formed much of Western civilization. That passing era has been captive to a concept of the church that had been primarily dominated by its church institutions, its ecclesiastical authorities, and its *sacralized* forms. As such, the church and the culture it dominated were not always friendly to critical inquiry and creative thinking about that challenged church's essence and mission.

Yet (as you saw in the preface) that cultural dominance began to fade perceptibly after World War II (though the first blush can be discerned centuries earlier with the intellectual movement known as the *Enlightenment*). But after World War II a pervasive self-sufficient humanism, a normative secularism, was the incoming tide, and became culturally discernable, i.e., a culture in which God and the church were less and less taken into account, or even close to a significant factor. A polite deism, or a subtle agnostic mind, became more and more evident as the human community dealt with its challenges. All that by way of some explanation of the cultural background for my *homebrew* metaphor.

It will be helpful to realize that the first-century culture of Judaism (out of which the Christian church initially emerged) was also a culture in which the vibrant mission of the children of Israel—that of being a nation of priests, a holy nation, and a light to the irreligious (Gentile) populations of the earth—was also one of shifting cultural influences. Generations of forgetfulness had followed their initial mandate at the foot of Mt. Sinai, so that those same heirs to the promise of God forgot their mission, and only clung to the promises of their being a favored people. Their worship became institutional, what with a grand temple and a priestly order, and all kinds of external observances, while, at the same time, the ordinary Jewish populace became forgetful of the mandate that God's design was to be written on their hearts and incarnated in their lifestyle and behavior. God faithfully sent a stream of colorful and eccentric prophets to let them know of their unfaithfulness, and of his unchanging purpose to ultimately send his own chosen Servant, his uniquely anointed one (his *Messiah*), to bring about a *New Creation* by means inconceivable to the masses of Jewish people . . . yet a promise very much pondered by the faithful of Israel.

That being so, "in the fullness of time" and into the realities of human history came Jesus of Nazareth, announcing that he himself was that very promised Messiah, and that he was in himself inaugurating, in their presence, that very *New Creation*, that *Kingdom of God*. It was to be a radically new, transformational, supernatural, and unimaginable reality. That Servant, that Anointed One (*Messiah*), appeared on the human scene, in the flesh-and-blood realities of human history, with a message and a mission that were "'off the charts" in implications, and it was countercultural to a fault. And, just so you know, that Kingdom of God would be referred to in the New Testament writings by such other designations as: *eternal life, salvation, New Creation*, and in some paraphrases as God's *New Humanity*)—they all refer to the same reality. As we have noted above, though that messianic mission had been prophesied (or foretold) by seers in earlier times (seven or eight centuries before the appearance of Jesus), it was so totally *other* that it was an inconceivable "mind-blower" to those who heard . . . except that Jesus demonstrated its presence, its authenticity, and its power by doing many humanly impossible signs and wonders in confirmation of his message. In short, Jesus was a practitioner of what he declared, in order to silence those who were challenging his credentials. The signs of the *Age to Come*, which he was both announcing and demonstrating, were to prove that in himself, and in what he was doing, God's *New Age* was invading this *present age*. Light was invading the darkness in a person: Jesus of Nazareth.

That was, in the eyes of so many skeptics, so outrageous that Christ's apostles would candidly acknowledge that it was "foolishness" to the intellectual skeptics. It also emerged as a culture-forming and transforming force among the poor, the weak, and the lowly born—among an unlikely segment of the populace—and not among the religious, the proud, the powerful, or the intellectual elite. A most unlikely message! And . . . add to that the awareness that Jesus was also to become a convicted and executed criminal, and an enemy to the religious establishment and the Roman Empire. In a very real way, God's Messiah came in *hiddenness*, i.e., in humility, on the backroads of a marginal nation, to address those hungering and thirsting after something they themselves could not articulate.

Ah! but there were those ordinary folk who immediately sensed that what he was saying was something that they desperately wanted to be a part of, so they began to identify themselves with what he was doing and saying, and tagging along to be with him. That ultimately became quite a sizeable following . . . but note right here: Jesus chose (out of a much larger band of followers) just *twelve* to be his intimates. That band of twelve disciples, to hark back to our metaphor, became the original *homebrew church*! Jesus needed a group small enough so that he could reproduce his thinking, his message, his energizing power, and his lifestyle in them.

That is an interesting factor, considering that in our own time the ideas have emerged out of a working group of the pioneers of our Information Age culture, whose ideas have ultimately become immense influences and successful companies. Those same immense companies realize that if they are to stay creative and competitive they must be "on top" of the culture, its needs, and its trends . . . and so must be continually re-creating themselves and breaking with past patterns. It is the dynamics of how they make this intention into a reality that illustrates our point here, like, how do you get from a provocative idea to a huge corporation, while not ever being content with the illusion of having "arrived"?

Note, then, that the vast church institutions of Christendom, of yesterday's children, have been slow, even resistant, to such continual and radical transformation.

Jeff Bezos of Amazon refers to the heart of that company as being in small creative working groups that interchange ideas and projects with each other and energize each other. He describes them as *two-pizza working groups*, i.e., that any working group that is too big to be fed on two pizzas is too big to be at the peak of its interactive creativity. It must be small enough so that each participant knows the others, knows their idiosyncrasies, their particular gifts and insights, their seminal ideas and thought patterns, and so to mutually form their insights into the proposals and action that would continually and ultimately keep the larger corporation innovative, culturally attuned, future-thinking, and competitive. That seems to be a general pattern in companies such as Facebook, Google, Apple, and others.

Please don't skip over the implications here for my ultimate goal of reconceiving the church according to the design of God. It never "arrives" until the very end of history (Matthew 24:14). It must always be versatile, mobile, flexible, and innovative.

But note: Jesus modelled that for us long ago. He never even came close to mentioning the founding a new religious institution. The New Testament never assumes a top-down religious authority. Jesus, rather, will say, "Where any two or three of you are gathered in my name, there am I in the midst of you" (Matthew 18:20). So, the question: Where does such take place? What does it mean to meet in Jesus' name? How is he *actually* in their midst? The metaphor Jesus used about the growth of his Kingdom was that it is like *leaven*. Leaven is a living substance, such as yeast. It is a permeating influence that spontaneously grows and transforms something, such as an inert blob of dough, ultimately into edible bread. That is how, often hidden from view and in the most unlikely circumstances, the church has grown throughout history. (That principle is what was demonstrated in the field of information technology with the Homebrew Computer Club.)

It is also what was evident after the crucifixion and resurrection of Christ, when his disciples were still captive to more grandiose visions of something of splendor like the Davidic kingdom of the past. But when the Life of God (God's own life and power) came to indwell and empower their human lives by the Holy Spirit, i.e., when the Spirit of God descended upon them during the Jewish Pentecost celebration, then their eyes were opened to a compellingly alternative plan of mission. The creation of the church would not be in a new institution, but rather it would be more like leaven, a spontaneously growing movement of life and power— person to person, house to house, a contagious versatile company in which all were to be dynamic participants, and all were to be equipped and responsible for the mission and the reality of the

Homebrew Churches: Small, Creative, and Intentionally Relational

Kingdom of God. It was in such almost out-of-sight communities that it fulfilled the leaven metaphor in a hostile political, social, and religious environment.

The church, as the community of God's New Creation, emerged and grew exponentially as the message took on incarnational reality and spread rapidly from person to person and house to house. The gift of the New Testament letters (epistles) speaks to the existential challenges of culture and political realities, of error, mistaken priorities, dysfunctional personalities, and all the stuff that confronted real church communities as they spread across the empire . . . and across two millennia right down to the present.

In the overall perspective of the church, the *homebrew church* would be only one very significant component of the huge mosaic of the global and historic church that has existed for two millennia in many expressions, often symbiotic, but its basic form is always essentially small, like in homes.

Our proposal is that of the *homebrew church* as something of a strategic reconceiving of the church for an emerging generation that is formed by significantly different cultural realities, and to a populace generally oblivious to much of the history of the church and its influence upon the previous millennia. Such realities make it prudent for us to stop for a moment, to stand back and look briefly at where the church has come from and the evidence it has left behind.

From its modest beginnings, the church has, indeed, been like leaven, and has permeated a remarkable segment of the human community and in multiple expressions and traditions. Just because we are now looking at a post-Christian culture, what with a permeating secular humanism determining much of our ordinary and immediate existence, does not mean that all that has gone before has historically disappeared, or that it doesn't still contain vital pockets of life and influence around the world.

Not only are the major traditions of Roman Catholicism, Coptic Christianity, Eastern Orthodoxy, Protestantism, Pentecostalism, and innumerable independent Christian expressions still present, and still contain the presence of that leaven spoken of above . . . but there are all of those somewhat hidden Christian colonies, those communal evidences of the ongoing leaven of the Christian faith that escape much (if any) journalistic notice in places nobody would expect. There are clandestine colonies of Islamic followers of Jesus, Hindu followers of Jesus, and more of such cultural adaptions and out-of-sight colonies that are seldom reported other than in oral reports from underground sources. But the church has left its mark and its evidences, not only in the institutions of Christendom, but in its cultural contributions in literature, education, libraries, universities, and humanitarian agencies.

Be aware of that history as we look at the culture of the emerging generation.

How do we explain the mystery of the attractive force, the leavening power, of God's New Creation, and hence communities of faith? How is it that the followers of Christ find, or are attracted to, one another? What would attract a person into some colony of the followers of Christ? What is the dynamic that transforms an indifferent agnostic, a secular humanist, or a typical urban hedonist . . . into a radical shift of priorities and focus, and cause that person to be drawn to others with the same relationship to Jesus Christ? There is, quite obviously, no one-size-fits-all answer to that question, but it does need to be addressed, and we do need to acknowledge that it is a mystery that expresses itself differently in every person who has ever experienced such a transformation.

Those six guys who were the Homebrew Computer Club had a common goal, and some kind of dynamic reality and vision that connected them (even bonded them) with each other. Somehow, also, the church presupposes some common dynamic (which we dare not take for granted in exploring the essence of the church). What is the entrance point, the necessary response, for such homebrew working groups? Jesus likens the immediate context of our lives as a journey through a *wide gate* and along a *broad way* that leads to "destruction." He contrasts that popular and somewhat normal way with a *narrow gate* and a *hard way* that leads to "life." He also presents himself as the *Door* that leads one to God, into God's New Creation.

To say, then, that journeying through life's immediate demands in one's autonomous life, and hiding behind one's demand for privacy, is the popular course for most. A person may be defensive, perhaps, questing after some sense of fulfillment, but too often determined by social, economic, and other inescapable forces that define that *wide gate* and *broad way*. It may, on one hand, sound *cool* to affirm that "I determine my own destiny, morality, and well-being without having to resort to some notion of God or the afterlife." But the reality is that, very often, hidden down there in the depths (or honesty) of one's consciousness (or subconsciousness, or metaconsciousness) is a vague dissatisfaction with it all, and a desire for some center, some authority, some creative source, and some ultimate goal that one has not found on the broad way.

The mystery becomes the more fascinating when we hear that vast diversity of stories of how such journeyers on the broad way have become alert to that narrow gate and hard way that leads to life. C. S. Lewis, who was something of an aggressive agnostic for years while on the faculty of Oxford University, could be found regularly arguing for his position with his Christian colleagues as they met in the local pub. In his autobiography, he tells of that frightening night in the winter semester when "I heard the footsteps of Him whom so desperately did not want to meet" . . . and consequently, in a profound conversion, he was to become one of the most influential voices for the Christian faith in the twentieth century. Or there is Anne LaMott, the troubled but very gifted author, single mother, and drug user living a hedonistic life off of a houseboat on the bay above San Francisco, who kept having an annoying vision of Jesus sitting at the foot of her bed on many evenings . . . until she finally gave up (in a colorful and somewhat profane statement of exasperation in seeking to deny seeing Him: "O, f—! I give up") . . . and became a follower of Jesus.

But most persons discover the Door of Christ, the Narrow Gate, in much less dramatic ways: something they read, or the life and love of a Christian friend, or a chance conversation, or an encounter with a Bible, or maybe a tragic death of someone close, or something unexpected . . . will incite inquiry, and they become seekers, and so turn aside from the broad way of the immediate, and pursue the narrow gate and straight path. They search out that knowledge of who Jesus is, what it is that he taught and requires of his followers . . . until, persuaded, they assent to the veracity of his promises and claims. But then comes the critical next step: the seeker has to forsake his/her cherished autonomy (or privacy, or attempt to be his/her own god) and consent to live henceforth a New Creation life, i.e., Jesus' own life, into his/own life. Now, this is the mystery. That act of willingness to be made new, and to have the life of Jesus somehow indwelling his/her life, is like having the *genome* of Christ implanted in them, that *genome* now forming one's thinking and behavior—the image of God's Son being formed in them.[1] Jesus also mandated that this is not a "private" thing, but is publicly acknowledged in a rite called *baptism* in which one forsakes privacy and becomes a public follower of Jesus Christ, his faithful follower.

Now, please note: that is the common power at work attracting one follower of Christ to another. The same life of God energizes each of them, and attracts them, and calls them to one another (those others in whom the *genome* of Christ has been implanted by faith) in a multiplicity of ways and in unexpected places. The result will be *homebrew churches*—where two or three, or a dozen, are attracted to each other in order to process how they are to, realistically, be the incarnation of God's New Creation people in the midst of the vicissitudes of a culture that seems apparently self-sufficient in its secularity. They need the encouragement and insights of one another. They each know that they have need the refining and stimulus and encouragement of one another. But . . . such units must remain small enough to have a dynamic, personal,

---

1. Anyone who has ever had surgery knows that before they are taken into the operating room they are presented with a legal *Statement of Consent* to sign, by which they commit their lives into the hands of the surgeons, with whatever the consequences may be. Repentance and faith are something like that.

interactive intimacy about them if they are to accomplish their divine intention and mission.

But then comes the logical question: how did this vast influence get lost? Where and how did the church get derailed? It is to that question that we now turn. It will also engage us in the timeliness of our *homebrew church* metaphor.

Chapter 2

Reclaiming the Church's Founding Purpose

The question that any inquiring might be expected to ask is this: "If the church was such a big deal for so many centuries, why not now? What happened? What's different? How did it get derailed? Why is it hardly a factor is so much of the culture that our generation has inherited?"

To preface our answer, it might be helpful to quote a guy who faced a similar question for a once-vigorous Roman Catholic missionary organization, which had not only "plateaued" but had declined in size and influence precipitously.[1] His ultimate conclusion was quite simple: whenever such an order, or community, *dilutes, displaces, or forgets* its *raison d'etre* (which he designates as its *founding myth*), then that order (or community) reverts to *chaos*, or to essential *non-being*. That speaks worlds to us. The church, as it has and does exist, does indeed get distracted, subverted, periodically moving into deadends, becoming stagnant or even immunized to its own message . . . but then it also often breaks out into new forms, or with fresh self-awareness, though this can be traumatic to those resistant to change.

---

1. Gerald A. Arbuckle, SM, *Out of Chaos* (New York: Paulist, 1966).

Reclaiming the Church's Founding Purpose

When the church was young, for those first several centuries, it was focused on the mission that Jesus Christ and the apostles had given to it. It appears to have had a very clear focus on its *raison d'etre*. It prospered and grew as it obeyed its original mandate . . . until it was one of the major cultural forces in the Roman Empire. That being so (and for other dubious reasons), Emperor Constantine professed Christian conversion and made the church the official religion of the empire. He endowed it, and encouraged all the accoutrements of the other pagan religions, such as elegant sanctuaries and formalized priesthood, etc. That shifted the focus, and so, for all the many centuries since, the church became complicit with the "empire" (i.e., with the dominant social order) and was, for all practical purposes, the official religion of the Western world, its continuance being somewhat guaranteed. It no longer had to focus on its Christ-given *raison d'etre*. It could focus on its places of meeting, on its liturgies, on its dominant clergy and on hierarchical propriety, and it accompanying institutions, so long as it supported the empire. That is not to say that all the while there were not those pockets of faithfulness, and colonies of those who were motivated by the mission of God.

Yet, ever so slowly, while the church's physical and political presence were somewhat dominant . . . at the grassroots its *raison d'etre* was ever so relentlessly being "diluted, displaced, or forgotten." That long period of its dominance has been designated as the era of *Christendom* in which the Christian faith was a major cultural force.

At the same time, there was taking place something of a cultural *diastrophism* (that shifting of the subterranean tectonic plates that tends to obliterate whatever is on the surface). That era of Christendom seemed to be dominant right down through the lives of our grandparents, though the tremors of the diastrophism became more and more evident in the early twentieth century.

Stick with me, guys! This stuff is important if we are to tackle our task of *reconceiving the church* intelligently.

After World War II one can see the last grasps, or the fading influence, of the Christendom era. There was the optimistic attempt to enhance Christendom churches, denominations, and church influence in society and politics . . . but hardly any significant grassroots attempt or equipping to incarnate Christ's mission. The *post-Christian* reality was inescapable. Those Christendom churches plateaued, but then participation declined, and a pervasive and subtle sort of secular humanism became more culturally pervasive. The cultural diastrophism launched us into a transitional period of *liminality* for which the church had no patterns—it was something like a "cultural whitewater."

Early in that period, however, there were those who did remember their calling, and whose lives were self-consciously inhabited and empowered by the *genome* of their new life in Christ, and who began to engage in creative enterprises of all sorts, in order to restore, refocus, and remember that for which Christ had called them. (Hey, we'll come back to that.) Those Christian agencies and colonies that were faithful to its founding mandate actually prospered.

Colonies of God's New Humanity in Christ: The Church

It is an essential presupposition for our quest here—that of *reconceiving* the church—to be persuaded that we, as human beings, are created to live in *intimate relationships*. At the very creation, it was God who was sensitively aware that "it is not good for man that he should be alone" (Genesis 2:18). To that end, he created for that first man a female companion, part of the purpose being that they should procreate a family, an intimate human community. And even though, in what followed, that intimacy was destroyed in the tragic quest of those first parents to be their own "gods," and even though they immediately began to hide even from one another . . . still, the psalmist will write: "God has placed the solitary in families" (Psalm 68:6). Hang on to that: "It not good for man that he should be alone." *We are created to live in intimate community.*

It would be totally inconceivable, then, that when God unfolded his eschatological (or consummate) design *to make all things new*, and in the coming of Christ to inaugurate that very New Creation in which *all things* are made new . . . God would not also (as a critical dimension of that New Creation) create a community of that *New Creation humanity* to be the beautiful, intimate, encouraging, and interactive colony in which the human need for relationships could flourish and be formative in the larger human community.

Got it?

We are created for relationships.

We are not created to be alone.

We are incomplete in isolation in life, and outside of a true community of others.

So, now we're getting closer to the *homebrew church* paradigm.

We have reminded ourselves above that, in the mystery of it all, somehow in the plethora of amazingly different settings and circumstances, and among a huge range of human personalities, God has called us through Christ to be his New Creation persons . . . and to be continually recreating us, both individually and communally, or to be the veritable demonstration of that *New Creation* as we are being formed into the very image of his Son. The community of such persons—the *raison d'etre* of such—is to be *the incarnation of the community of God's New Humanity*. It is so amazing. "In him [Christ] dwells all the fullness of the godhead bodily, and you are complete in him" (Colossians 2:9), individually and corporately. This is huge.

Yet, out of the forgetfulness of that church of yesterday, there did emerge those who remembered the message, those who were knowledgeable about their calling now in a much different cultural context. They had to be very persuaded of who they were, and to be very self-aware, not only of the faith and the community it birthed . . . but also note: they had to be aware of the present existential culture into which the church is called to be incarnate. The archaic remnants of the Christendom church began to fade (even if they were ever so highly endowed, as many were).

But here we are today in this challenging new culture, and with iPhone access to incomparable changes and discoveries, what with global and Information Age resources that are bewildering and exciting. The question becomes then: how to incarnate Christ's New Creation / God's Kingdom people here and now? In what form does the community appear? What is the communal context of our calling by Christ in which it takes on flesh and blood? Where are our relationships to be found and where do we help each other in this fascinating journey?

That same guy (whom we quoted above) who discerned the negative influence of *diluting, displacing, and forgetting* the church's *raison d'etre* also concluded that once that process had taken root in such communities, it was essentially impossible to bring about their renewal. Tired, stagnant, formalized, impersonal, bored, immunized church communities of *religious Christianity* inhabited by passive participants . . . are something of an oxymoron. That guy's challenge was that such colonies could not be *renewed*, but rather had to be intentionally *re-founded*, i.e., something totally new was needing to be conceived. And that's where our *homebrew church* metaphor becomes so *apropos*.

Homebrew Computer Club and Homebrew Churches

Those six early IT guys who met in that garage in Menlo Park in 1975 had all been infected with the mind-boggling potential that they saw in the early microprocessor. There was something just beyond their individual conceptual fingertips. They were drawn by the common dream and mission of breaking into the future, of suspending past horizons, of sharing their diverse gifts and encouraging each other and mutually provoking one another. They were content to be hidden from the glare of popularity. Failure was always a possibility. They were free to challenge each other. They did not seek permanence for their club, but sought only their mutual fulfillment in seeing where their quest would lead them. And . . . when they had achieved what they wanted to achieve, they celebrated and disbanded their Homebrew Computer Club and became the creative agents of a whole new era in information technology.

While they were obviously and undoubtedly appreciative of the resources in information technology that had influenced and formed them, they were not at all bound to the contributions of the past, or looking to make some improvement on what *was*—i.e., the currently accepted standards—but, rather, they were seeking together to discover a possibility for the future that was (as we have noted above) just beyond their cognitive fingertips. They were excited to share their gifts with each other in the quest for their dream of some still totally unimaginable phenomenon that would meet tomorrow's world.

Similarly, our quest here is to conceive of some context in which Christ's new life (his *genome*) in in you is able to respond to Christ's life in you and me together as we engage in our pilgrim journey through the realistic vicissitudes of our 24/7 lives. How and where do we find such a communal context? How do we become a transforming presence in whatever existential setting is ours?

The ultimate clue may be staring us right in the face in the New Testament writings. *Homebrew churches* might well have been the pattern from the beginning. Note: Jesus selected twelve (out of a much larger band of followers) to be his *disciples*, i.e., to be those in whom he reproduced his own life and mission through significant engagement with them over many months. Then, (please note) at the conclusion of his earthly ministry, he commissioned (or commanded) them to do one thing: "Go, therefore, and make disciples of all nations . . ." (Matthew 28:19). They were to engage in the very same ministry of reproducing the life of Christ in others, as he had done with them.

If you stop and think about it, that is as close as Jesus comes to defining his Caesarea Philippi promise "I will build my church" (Matthew 16:18). He's obviously talking about something very relational.[2] The disciples, right up until the post-resurrection

---

2. The Greek word Jesus used was a common term used to define any group of person called-out (*ek-klesia*) for any purpose, whether it be purely

Pentecost visitation by the Holy Spirit, had a vision of something much more grandiose and institutional. (That has been the *subverting misconception* of so much of the Christendom church in the intervening centuries, alas!)

Look at what happens after Jesus departs from them, ascending into heaven. His followers "wait" as he had told them to do, not really knowing what to expect. Then, after fifty days, there was the dramatic and utterly miraculous pouring out of God's own Spirit upon them—which blew them away—that got the attention of everybody. The result was that thousands became believers in Jesus—believing that Jesus was who he said he was, that he was in fact Israel's long-awaited *Messiah*, and that in him God's *Age to Come* had dawned, i.e., that *God's New Age* had invaded *this age*.

The immediate question would be: what were they to do with that miraculous new life they had received (and in the midst of a hostile religious and political climate)?

Project back, if you can, into that culture, which was an *oral* culture where few were literate, and where there was not even access to any such medium as that of hand-scripted manuscripts. The source of detailed information about Jesus' life and his teachings could only come out of the mouths of those who had been his intimates, his disciples during his early ministry. It was natural, then, to hear the teachings of those disciple-apostles in some public space. They therefore (according to the record) immediately came together in some public place (probably the temple porch) to hear and ingest the apostles' teaching, to listen to the word of Christ, and to get basic instructions from those who had been discipled by Jesus. What then? That was, mind you, demanding and life-changing stuff. And they had become, individually, recipients of God's new life, God's New Creation persons. That meant a totally and radically different conception of what life was all about. So,

---

social, or political, etc. It was in its later translation into early English that the word *church* was used which has a bit of a different connotation—meaning something like 'the Lord's people' which misses the missional, relational, and eschatological flavor of the kind of community Jesus was prophesying.

then, *where* and *how* to process that? How to engage with those others who were also part of that miracle.

The answer to that question couldn't be clearer. In the account of the immediate results of that Pentecost event, it says (Acts 2:42–47) that they continued, evidently, to have public time with the apostles, but then it spells out as the primary locus of their new life: that they met from house to house. They were together "from house to house." Don't miss the realities here. They had become followers of an executed criminal by the Roman Empire, and in a context of the hostility of the Jewish authorities. So long as they were able, evidently, they did gather in public to hear the apostles' teaching but then they got together from house to house. What did they do there? The record says that they "devoted themselves to the apostles' teachings and fellowship [*koinonia*, or intimate interaction with each other], to the breaking of bread and prayers. And awe came upon every soul . . . and having favor with all the people" (Acts 2:42–47). The brief description leaves us with the inescapable flavor of intimacy. None considered his or her possessions as their own, but shared. In homes they broke bread, they shared meals. That description can only connote communities small enough for such dynamics.

What did they do? They created the original *homebrew churches*. They ministered to one another, they shared their belongings and gifts, they lived out their new lives in Christ with one another in the midst of the realities of such a very threatening and difficult setting. That phenomenon was visible to the larger community (i.e., they had "street cred"). The communities were contagious. And that became the pattern. The fact that they met house to house and had that kind of intimate, mutually nurturing, and interacting sense of responsibility for one another meant that such could not be very large; the houses were ordinarily pretty modest among ordinary people. That, then, is the pattern for all the New Testament communities of which we have records. They were, ordinarily, churches meeting in someone's house. (They would fit Jeff Bezos's *two-pizza working groups* with Amazon!)

The Critical One Another Passages in the New Testament

It is puzzling, then, that in seeking to exegete the inner dynamics of the church there seldom comes one of the enormously enlightening components, so replete in those first-century documents. That component is one of the multiple instructions, or exhortations, addressing our mutual responsibilities to *one another*. It begins with Jesus' own: "A new commandment I give you that you love one another as I have loved you, so shall you love one another" (John 13:34). Those many *one another* passages spell out the relational function of the *homebrew churches,* as those communities sought to live out their New Creation lives, their calling to walk as children of the light, in the midst of this present dominion of darkness: ". . . let each of you speak the truth with his neighbor for we are members one of another" (Ephesians 4:25); "And let us consider how to stir up one another to love and good works, not neglecting to meet together . . . but encouraging one another" (Hebrews 10:24); "Let the word of Christ dwell in you richly, teaching and admonishing one another in all wisdom . . ." (Colossians 3:16); "Therefore encourage one another and build one another up, just as you are doing" (1 Thessalonians 5:11); "Bear one another's burdens, and so fulfill the law of Christ" (Galatians 5:2); . . . and, though not a *one another* passage proper, it is interesting that within the community there is also the responsibility of Christ's followers to rebuke and challenge another when their thinking or behavior deserves it: ". . . reprove, rebuke, and exhort with complete patience and teaching" (2 Timothy 4:2). We throw that last one in because anyone who has been blessed with such a community knows what an incalculable blessing it is to have the right to challenge, or even intimidate one another.

The blessing of such *homebrew church* communities is that they can keep us focused on our mutual calling by Christ. Their inter-animating dynamics keep us real and growing. They give us company on our journey as pilgrims and strangers. And . . . *everyone* is engaged in the ministry to the others (notice that there is no mention in the New Testament documents of church institutions, or church professionals/clergy!). There are larger informational public expressions for mutual teaching and formation in discipleship, but the focus is on the "house-to-house" colonies of mutual ministry to *one another*.

How large or small? Jesus said that wherever two or three were together in his name (by his calling), there he would be in their midst. And yet he limited his own band of disciples to his twelve intimates with whom he would be able to spend that significant time and so reproduce himself in them—which is our model for disciple-making.

Where do we find such others? Probably where you do not expect to. The Christ *genome,* his new life in us, resonates to that in each other. God's New Creation people are contagious. You may find such in some visible Christian assembly that tweaks your curiosity. Or you may find them in the neighborhood pub, or in some other kind of group gathering. Are *homebrew churches* exclusive? Probably not. In our global and nomadic culture, I may find such others in my workplace, or in my neighborhood, or in my running club, or on some humanitarian project—almost anywhere. Don't be surprised. Plus, there is always the effective instrument of prayer. And such relationships are long-lasting, even when they become separated over distance and time.

Back to our computer club: even though those six concluded their meeting in the garage after eighteen months, they were in touch and excited to report to others the progress that they continued to experience.

Having said all of that, there probably should be, in our experience, one primary *homebrew church*, however small and informal (even though in our mobile culture it is possible to participate in more than one). We cannot love one another with the love of Christ . . . in the abstract!

The ultimate goal of Christ's church is the fulfillment of his mission, which is succinctly stated in these words: "And this gospel of the kingdom will be proclaimed throughout the whole world as a testimony to all nations, and then the end will come" (Matthew

24:14). The people whom Jesus Christ calls, and in whom he lives, are not together exclusively for relational support, but are engaged in his mission to communicate his gospel of the Kingdom to everybody, everywhere. The church doesn't seek to insulate itself from the culture of darkness, but rather moves toward it, to bring to it light and the readiness of the gospel of peace.

Such Homebrew Church Formation Takes Time

The frequent references to the relationships, the accountability, the mutual responsibility that the followers of Christ have to *one another* (lest we take this too much for granted) *requires significant time spent together.* It requires a mutual ministry of nurturing one another out of the Word of Christ. It requires being subject to one another. It requires all those interpersonal dynamics with which we come to get inside one another. It requires confessing our sins to one another, and both rebuking and being rebuked by one another when the circumstances require it. It involves asking questions, bearing burdens, growing in mutual understanding. It even requires knowing one another's foibles . . . but in all, it has as its goal that all be reconciled to God and to one another in love, and more and more to experience Christ's true freedom.

That takes time!

It is also only realistically possible by Christ dwelling in you, and Christ dwelling in me by his Spirit, knowing, loving, hoping, and engaged in shared calling and mission. That is why the church is also called the *communion of the saints,* or the *communion in the Holy Spirit.* True *homebrew churches* are not mere chance clusters of relationally oriented folk, but are the creation of the Holy Spirit, i.e., "the dwelling-place of God by the Holy Spirit" (Ephesians 2:22), whether two or three or a dozen.

And . . . it takes significant time spent together, and time in which no one is passive or anonymous.

One More Helpful Metaphor Before We Move On . . .

In *reconceiving* the church for the emerging *iGens*, there is always the possible confusing tension between the larger Christian assemblies—the "together in public" that we saw in Jerusalem after Pentecost—and the smaller *house-to-house* expressions of Kingdom communities. There is a helpful metaphor that comes from a friend who was an aspiring mountain climber, and so chose a very high and dangerous mountain in the Rockies. He explained how the first thing you did was to find out who was equipping folk to ascend that mountain. So, what you did was to find a *staging area* at which aspiring climbers were informed about the mountain, its dangers and unexpected hazards of weather and rockslides, the physical demands, and the need for companions. All that instruction was done by veteran climbers who were familiar with the demands and disciplines of such. Those *staging areas* were the larger public meetings. Ah, but please note: the purpose of the staging areas was not to continually attend meetings at the staging area endlessly.

Those staging areas assisted the aspiring participants in constituting their *base groups*, or *base camps*, i.e., that smaller group with whom one would tackle the actual climb, and for whom one would be responsible and accountable, as they also for you. It would be the *base group* to whom one would be accountable, and with whom one would share the exhilaration, the dangers, and hopefully that conquering of the peak.

That's a good metaphor: *staging areas* (larger Christian gatherings to be equipped by the more mature veterans) and *base camps* . . . the *homebrew churches* with whom you actually engage in the mission of incarnating Christ's *New Humanity*, God's *New Creation*, in all the exigencies of that very real settings of daily life, with its pathologies, unexpected challenges and tragedies, or sameness and boredom of one's 24/7 life.

But we must *segue* now into some of the essential and *sine qua non* dynamics, and disciplines, that give such *homebrew churches* integrity and authenticity. (And, peradventure you are more confused than ever about where we are going, it might help to skip over to the Epilogue and see what we intended to write!)

Chapter 3

The All-Consuming Focus: Christ

The church has been around now for over two millennia, so that it should not surprise us that it can become distracted from time to time, or compromised, or lose its focus on why it even exists. Happily, we are blessed by having the primary documents of the church, from the first century, readily at hand in what we call: the *New Testament*. Those are the accounts composed by the eyewitnesses of the life and teachings of Jesus. They are followed, then, by a brief history of those first decades after his death and resurrection in which the church began to emerge. There follows, then, a series of communications from several of the formative leaders from that era, which provide us with the pieces we are looking for in our quest to form authentic *homebrew churches*. It is important to remember that all those first-century churches were, in fact, *homebrew churches*—in that they were all putting together "from scratch" communities around several essential (or *sine qua non*) components, which we will be investigating in the next several chapters.

It is also essential for us to remember that they were being formed in a culture that was under the totalitarian domination of the Roman Empire, politically. Rome's Caesar was the absolute "god." That was imprinted on Rome's coins. It was also a culture formed intellectually by the hugely influential philosophical input of the former Grecian domination of the world, and by Greece's great philosophers: Aristotle, Plato, Socrates, and a host of others. Those Grecian giants still dominated the intellectual world. Plus, every locality had a host of its own religions. The moral and ethical climate were determined by whatever the dominant order of that locality might be. Sexual and domestic norms tended to be patriarchal and permissive. Slavery was quite acceptable (the slaves of that day tended to be gifted captives from dominated peoples, or those who sold themselves into slavery to satisfy financial debts). Trade (or craft) guilds seem to have had something of a controlling presence, also. That all being so, the introduction of such an audacious new religion with its absolute truth claim—one that challenged the whole existing order with its practice—was dangerous, to say the least. There had to be something compelling to cause those early followers of Christ to risk everything, so as to identify themselves with the communal incarnation of such.

Just to insert a comparison here (and by way of contrast), our twenty-first-century North American culture has become somewhat immunized to the Christian faith, and to the ostensible Christian churches, and so indulges them while at the same time also marginalizing their influence. We are a culture dominated more likely with something like a *normative secularism*, and willing conformity to whatever the dominant social order of the moment might be.

But back to those primary documents. The inescapable and irresistible focus of those emerging church communities across Asia Minor, in Greece, and in Rome was that *the person of Jesus Christ was the all-consuming focus*. He was, according to those documents, the very center of time and eternity, the reason that it all existed. In him the mystery hidden from the ages was made known. What makes that all the more awesome is that the claim that such a peasant, that itinerant teacher, that executed criminal . . . *was actually God made flesh and blood*. That being so, the early church candidly acknowledged that this sounded like foolishness to the Greeks, and was a stumbling block to the Jews (the religious). At the same time, it was so compelling to his followers that

The All-Consuming Focus: Christ

they were willing to lose their lives for the sake of Jesus Christ and for his purpose (mission), which was to inaugurate God's New Creation (the Kingdom of God) in the here and now.

One of those disciples of Jesus was John, and his is one of the eyewitness accounts of the life of Jesus. John seems to write it with the Greek mind in view. He opens his account with the all-embracing (maybe cosmic) perspective of Jesus as the *word of explanation* of all things. To do this he employs the Greek word *logos*, which is translated into English as *word*, but which in Greek has the flavor of the *interpreting word of explanation* (or something like that).

Get this: "In the beginning was the Word, and the Word was with God, and the Word was God. He was in the beginning with God. All things were made through him, and without him was not anything made that was made. In him was life, and the life was the light of men. The light shines in the darkness, and the darkness has not overcome it. . . . And the Word became flesh and dwelt among us, and we have seen his glory, glory as of the only Son from the Father full of grace and truth" (John 1:1–5, 14). The inescapable conclusion to that understanding is that no individual follower of Jesus, or colony of believers, can have any credibility if that reality portrayed by John is not their *all-consuming focus*.

But the most of our primary documents are letters written by the early apostle-missionary and church planter Paul. Paul (who had, previous to his conversion, been called Saul from Tarsus) had been one of the early vicious Jewish zealots who was consumed with rage and hatred against the early followers of Jesus, against those who had declared him as the long-awaited Jewish *Messiah*. The huge and rapid growth of the infant community of Jesus' followers, in the aftermath of the resurrection of Jesus, had disrupted the Jewish hegemony and Paul was determined to stamp it out.

Ah, but on his journey to Damascus to capture and imprison early Christians, he had a totally unexpected, miraculous, and traumatic encounter with a vision of the risen Christ, the very one whose influence he was out to destroy. That inescapably real encounter with the risen Jesus Christ left him temporarily blind and helpless . . . and completely convinced. He was, to put it mildly, totally transformed by that encounter with Jesus, that very one whom he was persecuting . . . and it left him profoundly and passionately converted to Jesus. In those immediate days following that encounter Jesus communicated to Paul that henceforth his mission was to go and turn persons from darkness to light and from the power of Satan to God—to plant colonies of Christ's followers across many nations.

It is to this planter of those initial *homebrew churches* that we now must turn to see how unequivocal he was in making Jesus the all-consuming focus . . . and doing it in the particular cultural contexts, and in the midst of the customs that defined those contexts. Maybe a *potpourri* of Paul's teachings that were sent to those (often clandestine) churches will help in realizing that focus. To the church in Colosse, in Asia Minor (now Turkey), he wrote: "He [Jesus] is the image of the invisible God, the firstborn of all creation. For by him all things were created, in heaven and on earth, visible and invisible . . . And he is before all things, and in him all things hold together . . . For in him all the fullness of God was pleased to dwell" (Colossians 1:15–17, 19). Or to the church at Ephesus: "In him we have redemption through his blood, the forgiveness of our trespasses . . . making known to us the mystery of his will, according to his purpose which he set forth in Christ, as a plan for fullness of time, to unite all things in him, things in heaven and things on earth" (Ephesians 1:7, 9–10).

You catch our drift here: the church is not a merely human religious institution. It is, rather, the creation by Christ, and in Christ, of a whole *New Humanity*, of which those colonies of that New Humanity are its local expression. Again, to reiterate, the church is inconceivable apart from its all-consuming focus on that One who has brought it into being—at such unimaginably great cost—and who inhabits it by his Spirit, so that it can be designated as "the dwelling place of God by the Spirit" (Ephesians 2:22) and that communal incarnation of God's design in New Creation. The church is the present and flesh-and-blood evidence of God's reconciling love, i.e., God's glory, even as Jesus Christ, who inhabits it, is God's glory.

When Jesus was in the final days before his arrest and execution, he prayed an awesome prayer in which he said to his Father that he had finished the work that he came to do, his crucifixion was inevitable, and he was praying for those who were his disciples (the original *homebrew church*). He said to his Father: "I have glorified you on earth . . . The glory that you have given me, I have given them" (John 17:4, 22). The church, only by and through Jesus Christ, is that demonstration of the divine nature of God in the recreated human community. That was Christ's *eschatological purpose*: to make all things new—significantly, in the community of his followers.

For us, it is totally essential, then, that to even begin to conceive of any communal expression of God's New Creation in Christ we must begin with and be continually consumed by its focus on Jesus Christ. All that follows in the coming pages must come back to this primary *sine qua non*, this "lodestar" that keeps the church on course.

And yet . . . again and again, that essential reality gets *displaced, diluted, or forgotten* as we noted earlier. Already toward the end of the first century there is recorded in the last book of the New Testament (Revelation 2–3), in messages communicated to an assortment of seven churches in Asia Minor, how quickly some had succumbed to those influences that compromised their authenticity. Those seven letters are very illuminating. Some churches had gotten compromised by false teachers. Others had become comfortable and congenial, but had left Jesus outside the gate. Others had been distracted by pathological personalities. Only the couple of churches who were suffering persecution seemed to have their total focus on Jesus Christ because of the stark and ultimate choices they had to make—willingness to lose their lives for Christ's sake and the gospels.

In the centuries that followed, much of the distraction in the *Christendom era* was the church's proclivity to put its focus on its institutional forms, or on its creation of a "clergy" class of church professionals, or its ecclesiastical prestige, or on its liturgical rites . . . all of which too often shifted its focus away from its true foundation, Jesus Christ, who is always to be its all-consuming passion.

And Yet There Is a Focus within That Focus: The Centrality of the Cross

Over these many intervening centuries since those initial *homebrew (house) churches* of the first generations, the church's focus on it message is often found in its hymns, it's musical expressions. We hear that focus eloquently stated often in our Christmas celebrations in the hymn "Joy to the World" . . . "the Lord has come, let earth receive her king."[1]

At the same time, there is another theme within that one that can only be described as a focus within that focus. Take, for instance, the hymn, "Alas, and Did My Savior Bleed,"[2] which contains the verse: "Well might the sun in darkness hide, and shut his glories in, when God the mighty Maker died for man the creature's sin." Admittedly, that might sound strange to ears unaccustomed to Christian traditions, but it speaks of the fact that the church was built upon the reality of God's expression of his infinite love for his rebel creation by sending his Son to effect a reconciliation by becoming the one who bore the consequences of humankind's alienation from God, and vice versa.

That opens the door to all kinds of awesomely huge conceptions that are only understood out of the biblical narrative . . . such as the mystery of a God who reveals himself as one God, but existing in a community of three persons: Father, Son, and Holy Spirit. It also opens the door to our awareness that from earliest days God expressed his love for his people, and provided a way

1. Isaac Watts, 1719.
2. Isaac Watts, 1707.

The All-Consuming Focus: Christ

for them to acknowledge their inability to be what they were created to be—what is designated as: *sin*, or "falling short of God's purpose, his glory." Early in the history of the unfolding of God's design, in love, for this human community, there was the provision of animal sacrifices, in which a spotless lamb was offered in an annual rite of dealing with the estrangement and the guilt of the creatures against the Creator, and against one another. But those annual sacrifices were only the imperfect preview of God's ultimate design in dealing with the guilt and estrangement, which would ultimately be revealed at the coming of Jesus, as the Son of God, as the Word made flesh and blood (as we noted above), and as the Lamb of God.

Then, even though that incomprehensible act of God's love had been prophesied for centuries before Jesus arrived on the human scene, it was, until it actually occurred, not registering with his most intimate followers. They could not begin to grasp what the above hymn states: "when God the mighty Maker died for man the creature's sin." It was only after Jesus was arrested, beaten, executed cruelly, was abandoned by God, and died . . . and then physically and publicly rose again, and revealed himself to his unbelieving disciples, that such a *focus* (the cross) *within the focus* (of God becoming flesh and blood in Jesus) became the heart of the church's faith and message.

So, take heart. If our readers are bewildered, so were his early disciples until it was inescapably before them in the physical presence of the resurrected Christ.[3] That all-consuming reality dawned on them only when the Holy Spirit came upon them at the Pentecost celebration in Jerusalem, and became the major theme of

---

3. For those unfamiliar with Christian Scripture, then maybe they are familiar with C. S. Lewis's *Chronicles of Narnia,* in which early on there is an encounter between the White Witch (the personification of evil) and Aslan the lion, in which Aslan chooses to take the place of Edmund (who had betrayed Aslan's cause) and be slain on a stone altar, and so pay the price of Edmund's guilt. But, as Lewis explains, "there was a deeper magic from before the dawn of time." So, with the crucifixion of Jesus, there is a deeper magic from before the dawn of time that took place before the eyes of his bewildered followers, and has become the church's central theme in all the intervening centuries.

the church as it proliferated through the emergence of those early *homebrew churches*.

Check out some scriptures:[4]

> "Far be it from me to boast except in the cross of our Lord Jesus Christ, by which the world has been crucified to me, and I to the world." (the apostle Paul; Galatians 6:14)

> ". . . but God shows his love for us in that while we were still sinners, Christ died for us." (Romans 5:8)

> ". . .for all have sinned and fall short of the glory of God, and are justified by his grace as a gift, through the redemption that is in Jesus Christ, whom God put forward as a propitiation (or, sin-bearer) by his blood, to be received by faith." (Romans 3:23–25)

> ". . . And they sang a new song, saying, 'Worthy are you to take the scroll and open its seals, (i.e., the ultimate interpretation of human history) for you were slain, and by your blood you ransomed people for God from every language and people and nation, and you have made them a kingdom and priest to our God and they shall reign on the earth." (Revelation 5:9–10)

> "For the love of Christ controls us, because we have concluded this: that one has one has died for all, therefore all have died, and he died for all that those who live should no longer live for themselves but for him who for their sake died and was raised. . . . All this is from God from God, who through Christ reconciled us to himself and gave us the ministry of reconciliation, that is, in Christ God was reconciling us to himself and gave us the ministry of reconciliation . . ." (2 Corinthians 5:14ff)

Now, on to the pragmatics of equipping *homebrew churches*.

---

4. We use the standard English translations of the New Testament here, but if this is too strange to our readers, we highly commend Eugene Peterson's *The Message* as a wonderful and accurate paraphrase into more contemporary language and idiom.

Chapter 4

The First Gift: The Teaching Shepherd

So much for basic orientation about this *reconceiving* project. It's time to begin putting some flesh and blood on our *homebrew churches*. We are assuming (from the previous chapters) that they are, first of all, fairly small—from two or three to ten or twelve. We have also been defining the *church* as the communal dimension of God's New Creation (the Kingdom of God), which was inaugurated by Christ and is, in other words, his New Humanity. What makes these *homebrew churches* fun and attractive is that they provide communities of true freedom—that combined with relationships of shared commonality and mutual encouragement.

The questions, then, are: How do such *homebrew churches* come into being? How are they formed? What makes them to be something more than another merely human- association? How in the world do they express what the New Testament refers to as: the *church*? Super-good questions.

The answer begins when God *calls* us—and God's call can take on as many diverse stories as there are respondent to his call. In the mystery of it all, a person is called when he/she is made conscious (however that takes place) of the person, the teachings, the life and death of Jesus, and his resurrection, and so becomes curious about it all. It continues when that person hears Jesus' invitation, "Come unto me and you shall find rest," i.e., Jesus' invitation to receive her/him, and so, however you want to express it, that person determines to respond to Jesus' invitation, and in so doing to find true life in God. It is a new birth into a new reality. It is a mystery, to be sure.

Jesus unequivocally taught that he himself is the *Door* to God, and that one only comes to God through him. Entering that Door is an act, first of all, of *knowledge,* i.e., the knowledge of who Jesus Christ is. It is, then, an *acceptance* of the truthfulness, or the trustworthiness, of his offer . . . and it requires that *response* of our trust, that act of our wills, by which *knowledge, acceptance,* and *response* we enter into a whole new framework of life focus, of purpose, and of destiny (or meaning) as defined by Christ himself. That all may be quite sudden . . . or it may be the fruit of a long, sometimes difficult (even painful) intellectual and moral struggle that slowly results in an inescapable persuasion, all of which, then, results from one's encounter with Christ.

But then there is another—call it also a mystery, or call it a supernatural piece to this new life inside the Door—and that is: that there begins to evidence itself in us a new and different *energizing,* a different kind of power and awareness and motivation that is beyond our own merely human resources, and which one begins to understand is the working of the Spirit of God, . . . or we might say is the *genome* of the life of Jesus Christ, i.e., his resurrection life, at work in us, in our minds and in our wills. The apostle expressed it like this: "If anyone is in Christ, he is a new creation. The old has passed away; behold, the new has come" (2 Corinthians 5:17). The life and power of God's Son takes up residence in us as a very real re-creative energy.

And that is where the *homebrew churches* are birthed . . . when the new life in Christ that is in me is also, then, attracted to the new life in Christ that is in you, and in others, and by it we are drawn into a family unit, or into a communal demonstration of God's New Humanity, replete with his life, love, grace, forgiveness, mission . . . God knowing that it is *still* "not good that man should be alone" (Genesis 2:18), knowing that we need encouragement,

The First Gift: The Teaching Shepherd

and that we need a supportive community as we seek to live out Christ's radically new calling in the midst of the often confusing, hostile, demanding realities of our 24/7 lives, that context in which we are now "aliens and exiles" (1 Peter 2:11).

The question inevitably arises: When I come from the *outside*—from however that "outside" was formative in my life socially, philosophically, culturally, or just by some "go with the flow" mindlessness or conformity—to that *inside*—to the whole new framework of life and understanding to which Christ invites me—how am I to be equipped, or oriented, or made ready for such radical newness? And to whom do I look as a guide?

In answer, we turn to that remarkable early convert who became one of the early church's most fruitful teachers, and apostles, and models, and to whose writings the church has looked for authoritative answers, namely, Paul. Paul designates *four energizing gifts* or disciplines that the ascended Lord Jesus has given to his people, and by which to orient all who come from the "outside" to the "inside"—from darkness to light—in order that they may become mature and functional in their New Creation identity. Here are these four gifts or energizing disciplines: *apostle*, *prophet*, *evangelist*, and *teaching-shepherd* (or pastor-teacher).[1]

That is a good place to begin to understand the dynamics of our *homebrew church*. In this, and in the next several chapters, we will attempt to unpack what those gifts mean for you, our readers, . . . only we will reverse the order a bit, and look first at the gift of the *teaching-shepherd* (or pastor-teacher). It is also worthwhile

---

1. Ephesians 4:11. Perhaps a word of clarification is due here. The four gifts are all dimensions of the church's calling and essence, and though there may be, indeed, those within the community who excel in the exercise of one or the other of these gifts, still, even where there may be no one who is outstanding in the expression of these gifts, none must be allowed to be dormant in the church's incarnation. Interpreters of the four are often obscure or evasive as to how they are expressed. They are all to be part of the mature people of God and of the divine nature of Christ inhabiting his people. They do not always fit easily into some hierarchical church traditions, and are somewhat obscured by the notion that such are only expressed by church professionals. The four define the essence of the church's mission and maturity and all are to be equipped in the exercise of them. That is what disciple-making is all about.

to note that while these four gifts (or "energizings") are necessary disciplines for the equipping, or maturity, of God's New Humanity folk, there is no pattern given as to how, precisely, these take place, whether by individuals, or by some agreed-upon communal interaction—some nurturing relationship to one another.

Paul himself is a good starting point for us as he wrote to one church, "What you have learned and received and heard and seen in me—practice these things, and the God of peace will be with you" (Philippians 4:9). He would also tell another church, "Be imitators of me as I also am of Christ" (1 Corinthians 11:1). With that in mind, let's record right here: whoever is going to express God's gift of *pastor-teacher* (or *teaching-shepherd*) must also to be a model, a practitioner, of what he/she is communicating in the goal of equipping. Ah, but lest we let this pass unnoticed, Paul also describes this gift as a single gift: pastor-teacher. Notice also that he links the beautiful and venerable (in Scripture) role of *pastor* (which is another term for *shepherd*) to that of *teacher*. What makes that important for us to notice is that the shepherd (in Scripture) knows his sheep, and calls them *by name*—no anonymity, no "lost in the crowd" possibility here. While there is always a place for teaching in larger assemblies (staging areas), this gift requires that the person will know the name and face and story of those for whom he/she is expressing this gift . . . or if it is a communal discipline, the same holds. In our *homebrew church*, such personal identity is inevitable; one cannot be anonymous because of its limited size, i.e., the inevitability of a relationship of mutual intimacy.

There are several key Scripture passages that enable us to see this, i.e., that the dynamics of our *homebrew churches* are never *mindless*, and that the *knowledge* of the content of God's design in Christ for us is built upon that knowledge (never on some mindless spiritual experience), as the community attempts to find its way together, and to become oriented into the radical new framework of thinking and behaving that their new life in Christ requires.

The First Gift: The Teaching Shepherd

John 8:31–36: The Knowledge of Christ's Word Sets Us Free

Let's begin with John 8:31–36, which is anything but a *tame* passage (so fasten your seatbelts): "So Jesus said . . . 'If you abide in my word, you are truly my disciples, and you will know the truth, and the truth will make you free . . . So, if the Son sets you free, you will be free indeed.'" Wow! Does that ever open up a whole new understanding of who we are, of what is God's design for true humanity and for human history, and provide a key to interpreting the *stuff* of our daily lives, setting us *free* to live out our New Creation lives as aliens and exiles . . . and to begin to understand the place of our *homebrew churches* in that new freedom. We're free to come out of hiding, and to be free to admit that we are real "sinners." That initial confession of all the participants in the community is the great equalizer.

"The truth shall set you *free*" . . . yes, but that very freedom is also *not safe*. "Freedom is also countercultural and even revolutionary . . . it declares war on the darkness and all that demeans God's design for humankind."[2] It is that word of God in and through Christ which so transforms and sets us free. It is the knowledge of who Christ is, of what he taught, of what he promises, and of what he requires. We are the recipients of that knowledge of the word of Christ through our New Testament writings, recorded by his first-generation followers. We cannot afford to take that passage lightly. Jesus would also say, "He who has these words of mine and does them . . . demonstrates their authenticity as my true followers" (paraphrase of Matthew 7: 24ff).

Our lives together in the New Creation community (*homebrew church*, or whatever form the church may take) is *never mindless*. It is formed by *knowledge*, which knowledge then focuses us on the absolutely crucial role of the teaching-shepherd, of the pastor-teacher gift.

---

2. I want to give due credit to whomever provoked this concept in me, and I am prone to give credit to the late Liu Xiaobo, Nobel Laureate from China—at least I relate it to him.

Knowledge Is at the Heart of Our New Lives in Christ

Look at another illuminating passage that implies, inescapably, the connection of knowledge to our New Creation lives, and by implication the gift of the someone(s) who equip us in that knowledge. Check this out:

> May grace and peace be multiplied to you in the *knowledge* of Christ Jesus our Lord. His divine power has granted all things that pertain to life and godliness through the *knowledge* of him who has called us into his own glory and excellence, by which he has granted to us his precious and very great promises, so that through them you may become partakers of the divine nature...
> (2 Peter 1:2–4)

That's huge. Knowledge, divine power, God's glory and excellence in us, partakers of the divine nature . . . but the foundation of it all is the *knowledge* of Jesus Christ our Lord. Note the connection between these dimensions of our calling, and then feed into your understanding the crucial role of the *pastor-teacher-equipper* in equipping us for such awesome calling. It doesn't just happen mindlessly!

From a Different Perspective: The Equipping Role All Have to/with One Another

From a different perspective would be that responsibility that all who participate in the community have to be contagious with the word of Christ to one another. Look at Paul's letter to the Christians in Colosse: "Let the word of Christ dwell among you richly as you teach and admonish one another with psalms and hymns and spiritual songs" (Colossians 3:16). Then unpack that innocent-looking word *you*, in which mutual and relational context all are to be teaching and admonishing one another. Such a passage alerts us to the goal, which is that every follower of Christ has a responsibility to every other follower in their community of

The First Gift: The Teaching Shepherd

being so informed in Christ's word that they are able to teach and admonish, encourage and refine one another richly, i.e., to engage in the equipping ministry to and with all the others. But, again, such can only be possible in a community small enough (such as a *homebrew church*) that all have access to one another, and so that the communication between them contributes to the community's integrity as a demonstration of God's human community re-created in Christ . . . and that would include even the most recent followers—new believers have much to contribute. There are to be no passive participants, but rather all being formed and set free by the word of Christ, and so sharing that with one another.

It is worth pausing here to take notice that there is no concept of "clergy" in these teachings. These gifts emerge and are demonstrated from *primarily* within the fellowship. There will undoubtedly emerge those who seem to come to a more mature and wise stature so as to become leaders and mentors within the fellowship, but the responsibility rests with *all* to be able to encourage and equip the others. That is where the *homebrew church* form makes this mutual ministry conceivable, and as a necessary dimension of *reconceiving* the church for the emerging culture.

Formation into the Image of God's Son

Often overlooked is a very illuminating (or mind-blowing) component, or perspective, on the implications and goal of God's calling us to Christ. That ultimate goal of our calling is mentioned in several passages, and that goal is God's design from all eternity. It states that those whom God calls through his Son are to be are to be formed into *the image of the Son*, and that is clearly spelled out in at least three specific components: *righteousness*, *holiness*, and *knowledge*.[3]

---

3. See Romans 8:29; Ephesians 4:24; and Colossians 3:10. We focus here on *knowledge*, but *righteousness* pertains to the behavior of those called to be that of God's design, and *holiness* would focus on our reconciled relationship of intimacy with the Trinitarian community.

Sounds good, but what are the dynamics that make such happen? How are we to learn what those components entail? How are they to be incarnated in us? Who teaches and models and mentors us into such a formation? If this is God's design in calling us to be his New Humanity, then we must, first of all, be encouraged to put off the old humanity, but then we must put on the New Humanity, and so be formed into the veritable image of the Son . . . and that cannot ever be reduced to an elective! That is the very goal and design of our calling. Those are the crucial components of New Creation lives, and so of our New Humanity. Those determine how we become the salt of the earth and the light of the world.

Focusing on the *knowledge* component, then, leads us to think deeply into what the apostle was conveying when he said that we have "the *mind of Christ*," or "the *mind of the Spirit*" (1 Corinthians 2:16; Romans 8:6), or again, as one paraphrase graphically states it, ". . . *that you may see, as it were, all things from God's point of view*" (J. B. Phillips on Colossians 1:9–10). That compels us to look again at the gift of the *teaching-shepherd* as so very essential to the whole project of creating true Christian community. God's New Humanity is to be conformed to the Son of God in *knowledge*.

Two Examples: The Church in Jerusalem and the Church in Ephesus

Our need of teaching-shepherds, or pastor-teachers, who are to be mentors and practitioners of that which they are teaching (nearly always in very non-ideal contexts), emerges in our own quest in this book to discern the *form* of such colonies of God's New Humanity. We need *models* of those who have fruitfully demonstrated what we are calling *homebrew churches*. The first reality to put in place, then, is that the first-century church was a missionary movement, so that *all* the churches addressed in the New Testament writings were, in essence, *homebrew churches*, i.e., small colonies of those respondents to the missionary message of Christ, however that had come to them. They had received the message and became responding colonies of the message, i.e., supportive communities of those learning how to live out that new and liberating reality that had become theirs through Christ. That said, there are a couple of models that will help us.

Acts 2:42-47: The Church that Emerged in Jerusalem

One almost needs a rollicking sense of humor to deal thoughtfully with this passage about the church that emerged after the Pentecostal visitation of the Holy Spirit upon the multitudes in Jerusalem. The whole scene was a total flip-flop of everything. Jesus had been publicly humiliated, reviled, declared a criminal, and horribly executed only a few weeks previous to this account. Subsequently, he had been visibly raised from the dead, to the amazement of even his most intimate followers, and even though he had spent several weeks with them they were still bewildered and confused about where they were to go from there. The risen Christ would only tell them to *wait* in Jerusalem, and that they would shortly receive the power of the Holy Spirit . . . which also didn't make much sense to them. Then Jesus ascended up to heaven, disappeared out of their sight . . . and there they were, on their own. So, they waited. They reminded themselves of all he had taught them. The context in Jerusalem was still hostile, and the Jewish community was eager to have done with that troublesome movement.

But then . . . fifty days after the Passover feast (at which feast Jesus had been executed) there took place the Jewish festival of Pentecost. That celebration attracted to Jerusalem a vast international crowd of Jews. It was there, right in the middle of that celebration, astoundingly, that the Holy Spirit, whom Jesus had promised, descended publicly, dramatically, and miraculously upon the company of Christ's disciples with all kinds of displays of signs and wonders. The disciples, so energized by that power of the Spirit, and so compelled, rushed out to explain and declare to the crowds the message, namely, that Jesus, whom they had crucified, was in fact their long-awaited Messiah. One of the miracles of that occasion was that all the Pentecostal pilgrims heard the message of Jesus as Messiah *in their own language*. The result? Thousands became believers on the spot, and were baptized.

That, by the way, is the first call for humor: how in the world do you baptize three thousand people in a place where water was scarce? The sheer logistics of it all is fun to contemplate. But then, what do you do with all of those who had been converted when you are without any previous organization? Here they were, all those people who had repented of their rejection of Jesus, but now had received him as both Lord and Messiah (in defiance of the Jewish hierarchy), and who had his *genome* of new life take up formative residence in their lives . . . what then?

Here our pattern begins to emerge. The infant church begins to emerge quite simply. The apostles (and probably assisted by that larger company of Christ's followers from his earthly career) taught the crowds daily in some public venue (some *staging area*), so that the word of Christ was communicated to them by those who had been with Christ. Note: theirs was an *oral* culture. There were, at that time, no written documents, no Twitter or media, just word of mouth.

That brings us to our text in Acts 2, which in turn brings us to the basic form of the church: *they met in homes* to process it all. They were together in homes, and engaged *in the apostles' doctrine, in intimate community (fellowship), in the breaking of bread, and in prayers* (Acts 2:42–47). The new believes found each other. They accepted their responsibility for each other. They became those among whom the word of Christ was dwelling richly . . . and that, mind you, was right in the midst of the continuing resentment and hostility of the dominant Jewish order of the city. They shared their possessions. They were responsible for each other. And the account says that those house churches (or, in our term, *homebrew churches*) met daily. They needed each other in order to be able process this new framework, and to deal with the realities. It was all so new and they were so vulnerable. They were watching their Lord Jesus actually building his church, as he said he would. They engaged in their missionary calling by him contagiously, which is evidenced in that the early records tell us that the Lord was adding to their number daily and exponentially those being saved . . . even Jewish priests were being saved (Acts 6:7).

Two forms of the teaching-shepherd are in evidence here. First, there was the public teaching of the word of Christ by the apostles, and then, secondly, there were the functioning New Creation communities meeting daily in the homes of the Jerusalem believers, where they processed it all with each other. It all begins to come into focus for us, i.e., small colonies being equipped to be the flesh-and-blood incarnation of the life of Christ, of God's New Humanity. The knowledge of Christ, the "sweet aroma of Christ," permeated Jerusalem. They would daily articulate the word of Christ and relate it all to Jesus' mission, which mission was to inaugurate his *Age to Come*, the *Kingdom of God*, God's *New Creation*. The initial teaching-shepherds were the apostles themselves. Subsequently, though, those who believed met in homes, where they processed those apostolic messages with each other, and so became teaching-shepherds-practitioners with and to one another. Undoubtedly, in time, some would emerge as more skillful, or gifted, in this necessary gift than others, but *no one was passive* in the exercise of this gift.

Then the realities of their radical new message began to emerge. They were responding to Jesus' message, and the freedom that resulted. That message was disruptive of traditional Judaism. The result of that was that it did not take long for the Jewish hierarchy to initiate the persecution of the followers of Jesus. That would mean that the public gatherings (which were probably conducted in the outer courts of the temple) became impossible . . . and the church would be meeting primarily in homes: *homebrew churches* in which small and intimate supportive fellowships processed the new life in Christ, and the mission to which they had been called, together . . . and each of those would undoubtedly "network" with others. They prayed their way into the formation of the newness of it all, and the incarnational challenges that went along with it. They probably only slowly began to realize and become self-conscious of how countercultural and radical they were.

Yet . . . the church was growing exponentially, and new colonies of believers began to be birthed in adjoining towns and cities, and to leap over national and ethnic boundaries, and to spread over the Roman world (which will be the subject of our next chapter on the gift of *apostle*).

Acts 19: 1–10 and 20:20: From Ephesus to All Asia Minor

These two companion passages give us an account of the church moving out of Jerusalem and Palestine and into adjoining countries. It is the account of Paul's missionary journey as a church planter into Ephesus, and then his later reflection on that planting. It is most instructive in many ways. We visited Paul's transforming conversion above, but it is worth revisiting here, by way of explanation to our readers who are not familiar with all the background here. The focus is Paul, who had been an erudite Jew, a rising star in Jewish leadership, and a zealot among those seeking to obliterate this troublesome new sect of Jesus' followers. But in a dramatic (and maybe amusing) way, he was converted dramatically in an unexpected encounter with the living Lord Jesus Christ, whom he hated, i.e., he was knocked off his horse and blinded by a bright light while on one of his missions to imprison and persecute the followers of Jesus in Damascus. Subsequently, after some initial engagement with the Christian leaders in Jerusalem, he disappeared for an extended and mysterious time alone with Jesus in some remote spot. That period was obviously so intense that he seldom gave us clues about all that happened, except that he had all his systems totally reprogramed, and his vast intellectual grasp of Jewish scriptures so reinterpreted around their fulfillment in Jesus as Messiah, and he matured into a giant teaching and mentoring personality, and missionary to the unreached across the world. He was subsequently affirmed by the apostles in Jerusalem, and given their blessing to be a spokesperson for the church. He was to become the church's most prominent missionary, and the author of

The First Gift: The Teaching Shepherd

the majority of the written documents of the New Testament. So much for background . . .

One of his missionary journeys took him to the seaport city and commercial center of Ephesus, in Asia Minor. In that episode, as it is recorded, Paul came to that city in which he somehow he found some followers of Christ (the fruit of a former missionary named Apollos). What he quickly discerned, as he questioned them, was that Apollos had not taught them about the essential role of the Holy Spirit in creating new life in them. Thereupon, Paul filled them in, laid hands upon them, and the Holy Spirit came upon them dramatically. There were twelve of those who became Christ's followers. What then? He, being a Jew, went to the synagogue and for several months engaged in conversations in which he explained Jesus and the Kingdom of God. That was alright for a while, but the leaders of the synagogue became restive, so Paul took the believers apart into a rented hall . . . and note: he became their teaching-shepherd, their pastor-teacher, for two years. He brought them to maturity in Christ as agents of the mission of Christ. He formed them in the knowledge of Jesus and the Kingdom. In his later reflection, he would later report that he taught them in Ephesus, in public and from house to house.

The result? ". . . that all the residents of Asia [Minor] heard the word of the Lord" (Acts 20:10). From twelve in Ephesus to all of Asia Minor! We must not rush past that report. How in the world did that happen? It happened because Ephesus was a commercial center, and those whom Paul taught and mentored were regularly engaged in commercial activities that took them across the subcontinent. And they, being maturely equipped in the knowledge of the message, and being contagious with it, in turn became the apostles, the communicators, to those with whom they were engaged in the various cities.

Paul knew that the role of the *teaching-shepherd* is to equip all of God's people for the work of the ministry in whatever venue the operated. From twelve . . . to the whole region. I love it! Paul himself didn't take the word of the Lord to those other cities . . . rather, he made disciples, so that in their engagement with the residents of those cities they could sow the seed of the word of Christ, and so form new *homebrew churches,* colonies of God's New Humanity. Disciples made disciples. But . . . they had been equipped by a gifted teaching-shepherd: Paul. They, in turn, would become the teaching-shepherds of those who responded along their trade routes.

Paul becomes, then, a good model for us in the exercise of this gift. Yes, the Lord who calls also knows that all need companions with whom to process this pilgrimage, and to have the word of Christ dwelling among them richly, and to teach and admonish one another—communities of true freedom, participants who know who they are and what life is all about in the light of the word of Christ. Being so equipped also frees them to live joyously and non-defensively in a sociocultural context that is typically indifferent to the word of Christ, if not downright hostile. They are free to engage, to listen, to ask questions, and to display love and good works to those who "blow them off" as weird, or weak, or as fools.

Caveats: It's Not Always Simple or Without Hazards

Before we leave this chapter, a word of full disclosure: I've been speaking in ideal terms here, laying out the biblical patterns. But, as anyone who has engaged in this calling knows, the territory is seldom neutral or predictable. For one thing, there are always emerging those false teachers who subtly distort the message, those charlatans or charismatic figures who claim to have some amazing new interpretation, and who draw away the ill-prepared into their new cult . . . not to mention that new believers have a way of often being messy.

In the digital age of the Internet, one has access on a smartphone to more biblical and theological resources than any large library—but also to more false teachings, alas. The Christian life is fraught with complexities and ambiguities. All of this is the reason the church has always claimed the scriptures of the Old and New Testaments as its final authority, its guiding line, its source of true

The First Gift: The Teaching Shepherd

knowledge, its ever-self-correcting *inertial guidance system*. Ordinary believers who immerse themselves in the words of Scripture (and, hence, the word of Christ and the apostolic writings) become the true children of the Light. We today are blessed with an array of really good teachers, however, and have all kinds of riches of biblical knowledge accessible to us.[4]

Yes, our calling to Christ leads us into all kinds of real-life experiences that are complex and ambiguous, into times of doubt and confusion, into encounter with pathological and deceptive personalities, into unexpected stuff . . . which is why God calls us into colonies of his followers and in which we find joy and hope and mutual refining and encouragement and support. We're projecting an ideal here, and we need others with whom to discern and process all the non-ideal alternatives. Our proposal of *homebrew churches* is one expression of the gift of companions for the journey that is God's design to keep us from being alone, so also there comes both the individual and the *one another* gift of those essential *teaching-shepherds* to equip us into a mature understanding of the word of Christ. But in God's design, all his people are to be equipped with this gift as they become mature in their calling. Now on to the gift of *apostle* . . .

---

4. Let me highly commend the English Standard Version Study Bible as such a source. It is a recent British translation of the Scriptures, and has helpful explanatory notes by an array of well-credentialed scholars from several nations who help questioners "over the humps" in their understanding.

Chapter 5

The Gift of Apostle

The gift of *apostle* (in which all of God's people are to be equipped) has "As the Father has sent me, even so do I send you" (John 20:21) written all over it. It comes with our calling to Christ, and is inherent in (what we have termed) the *genome* of Christ, in his DNA, which is the divine life indwelling our human lives as his New Creation people. It is that energizing by his Holy Spirit that expresses his mission "to seek and to save the lost" (Luke 19:10)—his own search and rescue mission. Yes, it is the *missionary gift* given to every follower of Jesus Christ, every *participant* in his church.[1]

This apostolic gift is *not* the special province of (what are often designated as) professional missionaries, though, to be sure, there will always be the need for those gifted persons who are called into unreached portions of the human community. Yes, and it is right here that the role of our *homebrew church* to equip, to encourage, to refine, and to hold each participant accountable becomes such a wonderful gift. For us to engage in the church's missionary confrontation with the darkness, in its confrontation with God's rebellious or indifferent creation, its daily encounter

---

1. The word *apostle* itself is a composite word in the original (*apo-stello*), which means *sent out*.

The Gift of Apostle

with those who are hostile to God's design in Christ . . . brings with it all kinds of dangers, complex behavioral and professional challenges, and uncharted new terrains for us.

Just as the Homebrew Computer Club, which met in that garage in Menlo Park in 1975, was composed of those six IT visionaries seeking to discover a whole new dimension pertaining the potential of the computer, which was just beyond their fingertips . . . so also the *homebrew church* is always to be on an aggressive mission to engage in Christ's mission to be the children of the Light in the immediate realities with the darkness of a culture, and of a society that is resistant to that Light (which society and culture will be the subject of our next chapter).

The church has been accurately described, by some who are faithfully engaged, as "the missionary arm of the Holy Trinity"[2] . . . and as such, none are to be passive, and so all need the resources, the encouragement, the prayers, the rebukes, and the accountability to the other in their *homebrew church*.

The God Who Calls Is a Missionary God

All that we have been saying here flows quite inescapably from the fact that the God and Father of our Lord, Jesus Christ, is a *missionary God*. When Jesus declared to his followers, "As he Father has sent me, even so am I sending you" (John 20:21), he was giving to us a huge insight into the missionary heart of God, which keeps surfacing from the opening pages of Scripture. It is there, in that primordial account of the creation, and then the rebellion of the infant human community, that God announced that it would be the *seed of a woman* who would ultimately and mortally wound the serpent's (Satan's) head. That enigmatic prophecy would ultimately become reality in the birth of Jesus. It would be by that *seed of a woman* that God would ultimately reconcile the world unto himself. From the first, God's design for his creation causes us to be made aware that God is not going to forsake his creation to its

---

2. I attribute this to Miguez Bonino, Latin American Christian leader.

own folly and lostness. All that only makes sense, these millennia later, as it would be out of Mary's womb that Jesus would emerge as the one who would reconcile the world unto God.

God's missionary purpose surfaced early as he called a Middle Eastern sheik by the name of Abraham (a "God-fearing" man) and made a promise to him that in his seed all the nations of the earth would be blessed (Genesis 22:18). Again, that missionary purpose surfaces in the history of the Jewish/Hebrew/Israeli community (or Abraham's offspring) when, through a series of historical events, God brought them out of their bondage to Egypt, and to the foot of Mt. Sinai in the wilderness, and made a covenant with them, and promised: "Now, therefore, if you will indeed hear my voice and keep my covenant, you shall be my treasured possession among all peoples, for all the earth is mine, and you shall be to me a kingdom of priests and a holy nation" (Exodus 19:5–6a). The clear implication here is that it would be Israel's purpose to communicate the knowledge of the Creator God to the human community by their holy and unique behavior.

God's unswerving missionary nature is displayed again after the Israelites had totally "blown it" as a holy nation, and were taken captive into Babylon. Yet, even there, God through his prophets told the people to "seek the welfare of the city" (Jeremiah 29:7) in which they were captive, what with all the dehumanizing, difficult, and seemingly hopeless circumstances which was their daily experience. Also, through the prophets there is the account of the handsome, gifted, and competent young Daniel, who so proved his excellence in the court of the emperor Nebuchadnezzar that he rose to a place of great influence . . . but who, in the context with all the temptations to self-aggrandizement that it offered him, chose to live out his faithful identity as one of God's holy nation in the very heart of the palace of the pagan emperor.

Still, the quintessential evidence of God's missionary nature is in the fact that "God so loved the world that he gave his only begotten Son" (John 3:16). That gift is the inescapable display of

God's infinite love for the very world and human community that had so offended him—love beyond imagination. So that when Jesus calls people such as we, and tells us, "As the Father has sent me, even so am I sending you" (John 20:21), we can only conclude that we ourselves are to inherit that missionary passion, which is demonstrated in this gift of *apostle*. Our calling, therefore, is to become God's agents of his infinite and unimaginable love, and of his design to make all things new in and through Jesus Christ. That thrilling news that Jesus heralded is: that in himself God's *future age* has invaded our *present age*, and that out of his unimaginable love for the world. Jesus promised that it would be when this gospel of the Kingdom, the New Creation, has been proclaimed to every people group in the world that he would return and consummate all things. That promise, then, puts his missionary nature on those whom he calls, so that no one whom he calls is exempt from it. We are *all* called to be a missionary people. We are energized with the gift of *apostle*.

The Obscuring Paradigm of Christendom

The paradigm that has determined so much of the church's self-understanding over the former generations has focused on *the church as institution*, staffed by church professionals, frequently controlled (for the most part) by ecclesiastical hierarchies (denominations et al.[3]) . . . all of which, in so many ways, have subverted the biblical pattern of the church as the *communal demonstration of God's Kingdom,* as his *New Humanity,* into which all are called and gifted to be participants, and where the life of Christ resides mutually and responsibly with one another. Such *one another* love is visible and costly . . . but it is *never* to be theoretical!

All of which means, of course, that I, in this book, am proposing a radical shift away from that subversion, and to a much more *relational concept* in which we are all gifted to be the Spirit-energized agents of God's mission, and in which mission we are all

---

3. Roman Catholic, Protestant (such as Lutheran, Anglican, Reformed), Orthodox, etc.

equipped to be the primary practitioners of the four gifts we are looking at in these chapters. Again, *none are to be passive* in that mission.[4]

All the gifts exhibit the *genome* of Christ. But just now I will present some helpful illustrations to assist us with this apostolic gift.

The Marketplace Ministries of InterVarsty Christian Fellowship

Since the late 1940s, the collegiate ministry InterVarsity Christian Fellowship had been sponsoring impressive triennial missionary conferences for their collegiate constituents, focusing on informing and recruiting collegians for the Christ's missionary mandate. It was called the Urbana Missionary Convention, after its long-time meeting place at the University of Illinois at Urbana. Over the decades it grew to a convention of over 18,000 participants.

Then in 1987 one of the convention's senior staff, Pete Hammond, was responsible for the post-convention evaluation. It was in that process that Pete had his eyes opened to an illuminating conclusion: here were gathered these thousands of gifted young men and women, all of whom had a heart for God's mission . . . but of that vast number only a small percentage would commit themselves to missionary careers, in the generally understood concept of professional cross-cultural missionaries. But what of the rest?

Pete's conclusion was they would return home inspired, but with a subliminal sense of a kind of guilt, a sense that they were taking a second-rate course in their response to Christ's Great Commission (Matthew 28:18–20), while the reality was that they would inhabit one of the world's major mission fields, namely, the

---

4. There are other enabling gifts and practical gifts mentioned in the New Testament documents, such as the gift of administration, the gift of generous giving, etc. The ascended Lord gives to his church those gifts needed at specific times, and diverse circumstances, which also involves, to be sure, some quite miraculous gifts. Such miraculous gifts would include speaking in unknown tongues, healing, and miracles when the mission requires such. They seem to be for specific times, and temporary for the most part.

The Gift of Apostle

North American workplace! Thus, for several years, under a foundation grant, Pete was enabled to provide written resources and conference gatherings under the rubric of Marketplace Ministries, and to open many eyes to how one faithfully exercises his/her gift of *apostle* in that mission field, which was their daily workplace.

Similarly, the Graduate Faculty Ministry of InterVarsity Christian Fellowship

InterVarsity Christian Fellowship was founded to provide an equipping ministry to collegians on the campus mission field. It was focused primarily on undergraduates. Its founders sensed the inescapable reality of colleges and universities, and of their strategic influence on forming the culture. But as the movement matured, it also began to be aware of how much the faculty and the graduate students influenced the undergradates. And so emerged its Graduate Faculty Ministry.

At one of that ministry's national (actually with international participation) conferences, meeting in Chicago some years ago, there were gathered some 1,100–1,200 graduates and faculty. Displayed over the platform was a large banner bearing the challenge: "Following Christ. Shaping the World." Those several days were not without teeth. Regular "witnesses," i.e., practitioners from many disciplines, would give personal stories of their engagement, their challenges, and times of fulfillment as well as of struggle as they worked out their sense of fulfilling their missionary calling through their profession. There were witnesses by environmentalists, scientists, poets, musicians, etc. That was all given biblical context by daily expositions of Scripture by one of the world's foremost New Testament scholars. All the participants were engaged in what we are talking about here as this gift of *apostle*. The impact of those several days was tangible. Most of those participants had campus chapters or support groups (their *homebrew* churches) back on the campus to give continued encouragement and mutual challenge and refinement.

Such is what the church should always be doing, and what our *homebrew churches* are to be about: encouraging and equipping one another to exercise the gift of *apostle* in whatever the daily context and vicissitudes of our life involves.

The Christian World Liberation Front

There are so many helpful models of God's people demonstrating the gift of apostle. Another example of that would be that of the late Dr. Jack Sparks. Jack was a professor at Penn State in the late 1960s, when the youth culture in the United States was in total turmoil, rebelling against all kinds of strictures, against the Vietnam War, against racial tensions, against moral guidelines, and anything else that displeased them. In was also out of that period, and out of the renowned underground culture, that there took place the renowned Woodstock Music Festival, which surprised even the news media.

Dr. Sparks was a board member of another campus ministry, Campus Crusade for Christ. His cultural antennae picked up the awareness that Campus Crusade was reaching the campus athletes, the fraternity and sorority folk, and the well-scrubbed college students . . . but that nobody was addressing the huge number of the alternative and protesting and troubled youth culture on campus. His research easily discerned that the epicenter for that youth culture was the campus of the University of California at Berkeley. Berkeley was the scene of the free speech movement, the free sex movement, daily protests, and all kinds of aberrations from the traditional. Dr. Sparks's gift of *apostle* kicked in, and he took action. To respond to that mission field, Dr. Sparks resigned his position at Penn State, recruited a small group of daring staff members from Campus Crusade, and moved to Berkeley, where they rented a house, and fully entered into direct daily engagement with the radical culture. They took on the lifestyle of the youth culture, i.e., bib overalls, beards, and all. They became familiar with its vocabulary. In essence, they formed a missional *homebrew church* as a home base. They gave themselves the title of the "Christian World Liberation Front."

They innovated as they went along, doing advertised outdoor Bible studies on the library steps, engaging individuals in conversation, doing street theater, paraphrasing scriptures into the vocabulary of the subculture of their contacts, and engaged in doing open-air preaching, being bold right in the midst of the protesters and spokespersons of radical causes . . . and praying like crazy! And guess what? The initial trickle of respondents to their apostolic faithfulness soon became a remarkable awakening over those several years of their presence in Berkeley. Hundreds came to Christ. As in the book of Acts, God was adding to their number daily those who were being saved—and all who responded to Christ were immediately engaged in daily disciplines to equip them to be part of the mission on the streets, participants in the apostolic ministry. They were absorbed into the *homebrew church* of the Christian World Liberation Front as a nurturing accountability community.

When someone asked Jack Sparks how he accounted for that awakening, he gave a response that is apropos to our quest here: "I believe that where the darkness is the greatest, there God rejoices to work most powerfully." With that in mind, our equipping in the gift of apostle should include the boldness by which we move toward the darkness in our daily rounds, with the persuasion that we are there to be God's children of the Light.

Roland Allen's Missionary Methods: St. Paul's or Ours?

An early twentieth-century pioneer who insisted on the equipping of every believer to be engaged in God's mission was Roland Allen, a British missionary to China. Allen soon realized the outrageous impossibility of ever reaching the vast Chinese population with a few foreign missionaries. He realized that only if the infant Chinese church equipped all the followers of Christ themselves to be contagious disciples, and so to become a *people movement*, would the task of reaching China's vast population ever be conceivable.

He espoused this conviction at every opportunity, and wrote (what has become a classic missionary resource) *Missionary Methods: St. Paul's or Ours*. His apostolic thesis was not well received by many. The book essentially fell on deaf ears, or was resisted by the Western elitism of the missionary organizations. So, for a couple of generations the church in China was effectively dominated by Western missionaries . . . until . . . the Communist takeover of China, and its "cultural revolution" placed severe restrictions on the church, and declared as outlaw all expressions of the church that did not conform to its Communist agenda. The government also expropriated church properties and engaged in severe persecution of the non-conforming church members who were determined to be faithful. Multitudes were imprisoned in concentration camps.

What happened then?

The witnessing or apostolic church in China went *underground*, meeting clandestinely and becoming intensely focused on its mission, equipping itself for faithful discipleship in the most extreme of circumstances, and in its exercise of its gifts. It also celebrated its freedom to lose its life for Christ's sake and the gospel's. For years, given the closed nature of the Communist government in China, that church was essentially out of sight. When some were arrested, and sent to concentration camps to be brainwashed, they made those very hostile scenes the context of their Christian witness, since they had nothing to hide there. Concentration camps became training centers for Christian mission. The West found this out only after there was some openness (during the Nixon Administration in the USA). The underground church was contagious and articulate in the communicating of its message, and was an instrument of hope for its participants. But it was out of sight. Only rumors occasionally surfaced.

Yet, when China became more open, and when it was possible to do some research, it was discovered that the underground church (whether Catholic and Protestant in its roots) had grown exponentially and become, arguably, the largest Christian population of any nation on earth.

Plus, it had demonstrated inarguably the viability of Roland Allen's thesis!

Equipping in the gift of *apostle* for all who are followers of Christ is both a responsible discipline of the Christian community, and it is dependent upon the energizing of God's Spirit. Followers of Christ come to accept the daily (or 24/7) context of their lives as the setting for such an apostolate, or mission. For such followers, the *homebrew church* becomes the *base camp* (which we spelled out earlier). It becomes that relational company with whom God's people become both responsible and accountable. It becomes their support group, their company of encouragement and mutual growth and refining. Again, such a conception of the church is essentially *relational* and is the (provisional) demonstration of the human community as God intends it—God's *New Humanity*.

Such a conception becomes the more fascinating when one conceives the mobility and global engagements that are such an ever-present reality with our own culture. International businesses and travel abroad, ever-present contacts with immigrants, and multiethnic populations in neighborhoods, public schools, and colleges also make it conceivable that one could be a participant in several *homebrew churches* in the different venues in which one operates, and which could initiate profitable networks between such communities. Then, in today's digital culture, it is also possible to have almost instant communication with the others via texting or email (social media are too public to be useful given the intimacy required in the associations of God's people).

There will also be those continuing individual friendships and intimate relationships from former (and perhaps now terminated) *homebrew churches*, with whom we continue to have mutual ministry. Again, there is no *one-size-fits-all* inflexible pattern, but rather continual innovations on the basic concept of our need of such others so that we are not operating *alone* in our scenes of daily mission. In fulfilling their purpose, *homebrew churches* will be innovative, versatile, mobile, and perhaps often even temporary . . . but very *focused* on Christ's calling, and his mission, and on our mutual ministry to one another in the exercise of the gift of *apostle*.

A final word on this subject before we move on the gift of *prophet*. Whenever *homebrew churches* become passive (or preoccupied with other things) with regard their missional identity, of their exercise of the gift of *apostle* . . . they stagnate, ossify, and forsake their calling as missional communities. So be alert!

Chapter 6

The Gift of Prophet

The inclusion of the gift of *prophet* as one of the four gifts that the risen Lord gives to his church to equip it for its ministry, i.e., its apostolate in the world—and *all* God's people are to be equipped with that gift—does, indeed, conjure up all kinds of possible images and possible misunderstandings of precisely what that might look like. We think, almost intuitively, of the Old Testament prophets, who were an assortment of interesting, often quite eccentric, colorful, and persistent heralds of the message that God had given them. Prophets included members of the court, rustic farmers, the husband of a promiscuous wife, and other in-your-face reminders of God's calling of Israel. Their primary message was one of rebuke.[1] They all were sent to tell God's people, Israel, that they had forsaken their calling and forgotten their *Torah*, which was their founding constitution. Those prophets had all kinds of ways of rebuking Israel for its unfaithfulness, which rebukes were not well received by their listeners. They were often persecuted and scorned. And, yes, the prophets were often

---

1. Old Testament scholar Bob Ekblad defines prophets as *leakers*, and likens them to the Wikileaks phenomenon of Julian Assange, which has hacked government files and reveals/leaks information that the government wishes to keep hidden.

"futurists" and spelling out future events, and the promises of God for his people's destiny.

In the New Testament documents, the phenomenon of *prophet* crops up occasionally in the lists of gifts and ministries as though it were an accepted and understood part of the dynamics of the Christian community. You have, for instance, the example of Agabus, a prophet who warned Paul that if he went to Jerusalem there would be dire consequences. And, yes, in the book of Revelation you have the glorified Jesus himself exercising his own gift of prophet in his letters to the seven churches. There he spells out for them their faithfulness and unfaithfulness, their obedience and their disobedience, and reminds them of their calling.
That all gives us something of the flavor, or the purposeful role, of *prophet* in the formation of the community of God's people.

But my own favorite example, which may be a bit more obscure and yet more helpful, is the *sons of Issachar*, who, as described in the narrative, "understood [or discerned] the times with knowledge of what Israel should do" (1 Chronicles 12:32). The tendency of God's people seems to be never ceasing in their forgetfulness of what they are called to be in this world, as well as the very nature of the context of their lives. This example is so very apropos to our pursuit here. An often-memorized passage of Scripture is, "Be not conformed to this world, but be transformed by the renewing of your minds that you may prove what is the will of God" (Romans 12:1-2). That sounds reasonable, but when asked what this "world" is to which we are not be "conformed," it is quite too easy to succumb to mindless generalizations, or "spiritual talk" that doesn't help us very much in the realities of our daily sojourns.

Another helpful example comes from the field of *missiology* (the study of missions), in which a critical component of training men and women for cross-cultural missions is that of *exegeting the culture*, understanding the fine points of the culture into which they are being sent. Ah, but every follower of Jesus Christ is called to his/her *apostolate/mission*, and it is there that they are to be the incarnation of the mission of God in Jesus Christ. Every believer is sent to be God's *New Humanity* person in the specific context of a world that is alien to that *New Humanity*. This calling is never lived out in neutral territory, i.e., the context is seldom congenial to this countercultural calling. That is why, in order for us to *not be conformed*, all of God's people must be equipped for their engagement with the particular *world* that is theirs, to which they are not to be conformed . . . and they must understand its nuances. God's people are, in fact, *other-worldly* and a people of hope (which we'll look at in a coming chapter), but they are at the same time very much a very *this-worldly* people who know that they are to walk as children of the Light here and now. They are to "prove what is the will of God" (Romans 12:2), to be exhibits of their Savior's passion for righteousness, for peacemaking, for justice, for mercy, and for sensitivity to the poor and homeless and victims of destructive circumstances where they live and work. They are to demonstrate God's love in Christ in their 24/7 contexts, the multiple mini-cultures of this twenty-first-century world.

The Christian faith, as one Christian author put it, "is too wild and free for the timid."[2] It certainly is not a comfort zone religion. This also is not done in the abstract. It is not enough to post a Facebook statement of Christian conviction, or to do an online signing of some dramatic ethical declaration (though those have their place, and I have signed such). Words come easy, but consistent *New Creation* praxis is demanding and costly.

Look at the Cultural and Contextual Factors of Today

It seems almost impossible, if not downright insane, to attempt on my own part to *exegete* the complex mosaic that is our twenty-first-century culture. We no longer live in self-contained villages where it was difficult to be a stranger. We live, rather, in the mosaic of a global society inhabited by an endless array of subcultures, all if

2. Madeline L'Engle, *Walking on Water: Reflections on Faith and Art* (New York: Covergent, 2016), 40.

which are continually in a state of mobility, transition, and change. Every home is a basic subculture, as is every neighborhood, and every classroom, and workplace, and recreational association. The cultural expressions are endless. But that does not diminish the necessity of carefully *exegeting* the culture we will meet when we walk out the door in the morning.

Church institutions have quite too often created their own in-house religious culture (their "safe house"), with multiple activities, in order to keep their participants insulated from serious engagement with the cultures (and the persons who make up those cultures) of their 24/7 lives. The traditional church institutions of *Christendom* have also too often made peace with the "empire" (the dominant social order) in order to secure a place of acceptance within it. It is also unmistakable, in reading works on Christian spirituality, that pious individuals have often created their own *portable monasteries* of various spiritual formations, so as to protect themselves from any serious engagement with their apostolic calling within the vicissitudes of their daily lives.

Then, of course, the advent of the iPhone has produced too many (especially the younger generation) who have created a very cloistered world made up of their "contacts," with whom they share texts and Snapchats, but in which world they can tune out anything that is difficult or unpleasant, or be conversant with the knowledge of history, or of their culture, and so fabricate a cocoon free of challenges.

In order that we come to some very basic sensitivity of the cultural context of our expression of the gift of *prophet*, take a stroll with me through some of the components that are present in the post-Christian twenty-first-century context that is ours. Again, this is very inadequate, but is at least a "toe in the water" for our *reconceiving* project.

The Emerging Generational Culture

Look, first, at the generational factors, especially as we are sensitive to the emerging generation. Every generation has its own defining personality and is influenced by the cultural influences that prevail at its moment in history.

I have already introduced this above, and what I will be doing will be, admittedly, inadequate and a bit repetitive. That being so, it is the generational culture of the *iGens* that provoked this book. It is only when one generation is succeeded by another generation that it can be reasonably evaluated. That being so, we never get an adequate picture of a generational culture while it is emerging. What is being realized by those who are presently engaged with it, and those who are studying it, is the growing awareness that this emerging generation is being formed by a radically different set of cultural influences. One component is that the emerging generation is more disconnected from previous generations, as well as being frequently disinterested in the history that has formed it. It is the product of factors not experienced by preceding generations.

Let's get our designation clear: this generation is being referred to as the *iGens*. It is the generation born after 1995, who are the recipients of the invention of the iPhone in 2011. Theirs is a digital world, and life apart from their iPhones an TVs is almost unimaginable to them.[3] That has created all kinds of positive and negative consequences, such as increased loneliness and suicides. It has produced an unwillingness to confront ideas different from their own, and to forsake the cocoon of childhood safety. They appear more intent on delaying adulthood, and avoiding anything that would challenge their safety, than previous generations. They are more connected, and have access to more information than any generation before them, but they are also much less adept at true, face-to-face communication. Early studies show such proclivities among the *iGens* to include those such as being more disengaged from the challenges of and knowledge about the larger scene. Not only do they, on the whole, seem more disengaged, but also more cynical. They are less prone to serious intellectual stimulation, to the reading of books, and more dependent on the Internet.

---

3. I am indebted to sociologists such as Dr. Jean Twenge, Tim Elmore, and others for their studies of this emerging generation.

Having said all of that, by way of rehearsing the findings of sociologists who have made a major study of this generation, I am of the opinion that the sociologists tend to veer on the side of the more pessimistic and cynical implications of the emerging culture . . . while I tend to be more optimistic. To be sure, adolescence is always a disrupting passage in one's life, what with the emergence of puberty, the rapidly approaching and unknown transition into whatever adulthood holds. The iPhone phenomenon has given them a tool by which to escape for a while into an Internet world of their own making, what with Facebook, Twitter, Snapchat, and the rest. It is obviously a trait that this generation is seeking to preserve the safety of the childhood cocoon a bit longer.

That having being said, however, generations also have a way of being self-correcting, and of exhibiting surprising new potential that is often huge. This generation is totally at home in the digital age, which is already making colossal breakthroughs in solving medical, environmental, and formerly intimidating problems that are downright miraculous. This generation is already producing high achievers, athletic prodigies, adventurers, and innovating and potentially creative geniuses. I think we are up for more surprises from them. It is also they who, apropos to this book, will expedite the *reconceiving of the church* into more germane expressions of the community of God's *New Humanity*.

Yes, at some point reality will kick in and these emerging adults—maybe a bit delayed—will surprise us all.

Then too . . . remember that it is Jesus who is building his church. It is he who came to reconcile the world unto God, and has transformed pagan tribes and alien cultures, as he has continued to radiate his gospel of the Kingdom through multiform colonies of his *New Humanity* as they permeated the cultures of darkness like leaven. I'm optimistic.

Such cultural realities also make the *homebrew church* form of Christian community all the more germane and transformational for our consideration. There are no hiding places in such a *one another* community, and there is much more communication and mutual encouragement and refinement. Remember: God has said that *it is not good for man that he should be alone.*

Multiple Subcultures

Or, look at the multiple cultures many of us encounter every day. There are the ethnic and lifestyle cultures, with all the challenges of those, and the multiple nationalities dwelling in most of our cities, what with those many religions, and sitting next to you in high school. There are all the ideologies and prejudices that confront us, from arch-conservative to very progressive in politics and civic scenes, or in the dominant social order. There are all the psychological formations and genetic factors that are exhibited in those with whom we interact.

Perhaps more critical for the emerging culture is the place of early home life and disciplines, or lack thereof. Anyone who has ever taken a Meyers-Briggs assessment also knows how many shades of determining personality factors cause people to live and think as they do. But the list is *myriad*, and yet this is the very real world that all of us, and tomorrow's children, confront.

Faith at Work

To reiterate, there are few *safe* villages in which there are no challenges. For a few years there was a journal publication called *Faith at Work*, in which the editors sought out those followers who were seeking to be "salt and light," to be faithfully prophetic in the daily setting. This included filmmakers, journalists, executives of corporations, educators, research scientists, and so many others. The contributors were very candid and open in their confession of the temptations and seductions they faced that were alien to their calling.

Yet, *faith at work* is our prophetic calling in flesh and blood. Every day in high school, or college, or in the minimum-wage workplace is the context for the prophetic calling of God's people, even when it seems boring or inconsequential. Every one-on-one conversation over coffee, or policy referendum of a labor movement, or discussion in class, etc. . . . calls upon the believer to live out, or prove, knowledgeably, his or her conformity to the will of God. Conformity to *this world* is to succumb to the dominant order, to the norm of self-sufficient humanism, or perhaps, by choice, to stay passive and "safe" in the presence of the disdain or dismissal of anything remotely tainted by Christian principles.

This contextual dismissal of the traditional notions and institutional expressions of the church makes our *reconceiving of the church* project to be the more urgent in resisting such cultural dismissal. "This is my Father's world, and though the wrong seems oft so strong, God is the ruler yet," goes the hymn.[4] The *reconceiving* will certainly see the church as the community of God's *New Creation*, which community is a culture-creating phenomenon to be sure . . . but this is always in the context of the contextual realities of its mission.

"Seek the Welfare of the City . . ."

When the Jewish nation were to be taken into captivity by invading empires, God gave them their mandate through the prophet to "seek the welfare of the city where I have sent you into exile, and pray to the Lord on its behalf, for in its welfare you will find your welfare" (Jeremiah 29:7). Such a scriptural mandate is always germane and insistent upon the communities of God's people. It is of the essence of the church's *founding myth* (see chapter 2 above). Such a quest for the welfare of the city requires continual creative engagement. It requires careful listening. A marvelous example of this listening would be the late Lesslie Newbigin, who, as a young British missionary to South India, made it his practice to sit over tea with the Hindu priests and to engage them in conversation, to listen, then to study their sacred documents, until the time came when he was often more conversant with their sacred writings and

---

4. "This Is My Father's World," words by Maltbie Babcock, 1901.

cultural expression than they were. It also gave him occasion to quietly communicate his own Christian understanding, and to become very fruitful.[5]

The cultural context of our own expressions of the *prophetic* gift has many faces, many prejudices, and has an expected resistance to disturbers. That alternative understanding also reminds us of the continual, and necessary, discipline of repentance, of being formed with a new mind, and of not being conformed to the culture of darkness. A critical dimension of our prophet incarnation must also be the sheer excellence of our lives and work, and our love for all, even our enemies. It also requires that we clearly understand that this context is seldom a *black-vs.-white* affair, but rather involves shades of grey. Along the way, God's people and his prophetic community encounter other men and women of good will, of peace, who will join us in our quest for God's design.

The *homebrew church* intimacy and mutual mission gives us a place to refine such a mission, to measure the credulity of our lives against Scripture. It gives to others the authority to hold us accountable, and us them. It gives us the place to discern what is false, and who are the charlatans who would distort the community. In their prophetic calling, *homebrew churches* are a healthy context for both encouragement and refining of this essential gift of *prophecy*, given by the risen Christ to his church to equip it for its ministry in the world that he came to reconcile to God by his blood.

---

5. Newbigin's book *The Household of God* (London: SCM, 1953) would become one of the first serious engagements with the missionary nature of the church in the post–World War II era. He continued to challenge the church significantly for the rest of his long life, and is responsible for the fruitful discussions on the *missional church*.

Chapter 7

The Gift of Evangelist

We come now to the fourth of the gifts, i.e., Spirit-*energizings*, that the ascended Lord Jesus has given to equip *all* of God's people for their daily engagement with its daily context and routines: the gift of *evangelist*. That is the gift that relates to our ability to communicate the essence of our faith in Christ, or to articulate it thoughtfully, if and when the occasion arises, or whenever anyone asks us for an explanation of our hope in Christ. It is the *boots-on-the-ground* readiness to communicate the "gospel of peace" (Ephesians 6:15).

It will help to revisit what we have been pursuing in this project. Our purpose has been to *reconceive* (or give a fresh look at) the church with and for the emerging generation. To that end, we need to go back to the beginning of the New Testament documents, and to grasp how infinite and unimaginable is God's love for his rebellious creation, i.e., for those very persons who ignore him, or dismiss him as a myth, or for whom he is not even in their thoughts, or who are angry at him, or hold him in total disdain . . . but for whose glory they and all humankind have been created, and are designed.

The Gift of Evangelist

The expression of that love of God unfolds in his ultimate (or *eschatological*) design of making all things new, of inaugurating his New Creation (Kingdom), of invading *this age* with his *Age to Come* ... his intent to reconcile the world to himself, in and through his anointed Son and servant, his *Messiah* (or Christ). And what we have been proposing here is (take note) that the *church* is the communal component of that recreation of the human community as God intends it to be. It is the human community reconciled to God, and so is re-created to communicate and demonstrate the love of God in Christ: to be intimate, forgiving, caring, serving, and loving even as Jesus Christ demonstrated that love.

That awesome design first emerges in the New Testament documents when an angelic messenger appeared to a virgin Jewish girl, Mary (the Bible is comfortable with miracles, so live with it!), in Palestine to tell her that the promise given to her Jewish ancestors, i.e., that somehow the throne of King David would consummate in an everlasting Kingdom, would come to pass in the child that would be conceived in her womb. When she protested that she was still a virgin, the angel assured her that the child would be a miracle, conceived by the overpowering of the Holy Spirit. The angel continued to inform and assure her that "the Lord God will give to him the throne of his father David, and ... of his kingdom there would be no end" (Luke 1:32–33).[1]

Subsequently, another angelic messenger would announce to a company of bewildered shepherds (minimum-wage guys) one night, "Fear not, for behold, I bring you good news of great joy that will be for all peoples. For unto you is born this day in the city of David a Savior who is Christ the Lord" (Luke 2:10–11). Take note: that announcement is the essence of our *evangel*, to wit, that God has in fact invaded his own creation in order to bring great joy to all people. What unfolded with the coming of Christ is the substance of the gift of: *evangelist*.

---

1. Reader, take note that the non-believing world has always had a field day deriding the ridiculousness and impossibility of such a miraculous birth.

God does not intend that his love for this very real, and so often fractious, world ever be hidden! It is his will that it should be communicated.

To understand how that "good news of great joy" (our *evangel*) began to unfold, we need to take note of a couple of dimensions. The *first dimension* is: that at the outset of his public career, Jesus "came *proclaiming* the gospel of God" (Mark 1:14), which proclamation was that the appropriate time had in fact arrived, and that the *Kingdom of God* (i.e., God's New Creation) was on the threshold. Conclusion: *proclaiming*, or putting into words—in whispered conversation or public address—the reality of what was happening in Christ is essential to the task, and the content of the proclamation is to be focused on God's love for this very world in which we live. His intent is to be known, and for his mission to seek and to rescue its *lost* inhabitants to be communicated. That communication would include his promise of forgiveness for all the aberrations from, and violations of, his purpose in creating them. It would explain how to come into the new life which he offers.

The *second dimension* of the work of evangelist surfaces in Jesus' first appearance as he entered his public career. It would be his appearance in his home synagogue, where he was asked to do the reading of the scripture for the day, which happened to be from Isaiah 61. That is a major eighth-century BCE prophecy about the ministry of God's expected and promised *servant-Messiah*. That prophecy is to the effect that the Spirit of God would anoint God's servant-Messiah to proclaim good news to the poor, to proclaim liberty to the captives and recovery sight to the blind, to set at liberty those oppressed, and to proclaim the time of the Lord's favor.

All the locals were impressed with Jesus . . . until it "all went south." That took place when Jesus claimed that this very prophecy was now being fulfilled in himself. "The very audacity that this local boy should make such an outrageous claim for himself!" What, then, does that episode have to do with our quest to understand the gift of evangelist? In answer, what it unmistakably says is that the communicating of the thrilling news is not just a matter of

The Gift of Evangelist

words, but it is words authenticated by good works, by caring for the real and existential needs of those that one encounters along the way. That would be brilliantly displayed in the public ministry of Jesus and of his disciples: opening blind eyes, healing the sick, feeding the hungry, cleansing lepers, accepting the outcasts... and so much more. His good works also provoked, all the more, the curiosity about who he was, and it gave him occasion, or cause, to do public teaching about his Kingdom, about God's New Creation.

So, it was that even Jesus' adversaries could not gainsay his good works, even though they were threatened by his claim to be the *Messiah*. His love for the loveless and his good works also remind us, again, that his life and ministry were *countercultural* and *subversive* of all that was indifferent to human need. It elicited both curiosity and hostility.[2] The lifestyle of God's New Creation people corroborates its authenticity. Jesus spoke about this when he had laid out before his listeners the character of his Kingdom people in his Sermon on the Mount. He told his followers to so live that "men shall see your good works and glorify God" (Matthew 5:16).

There is yet a *third dimension* that is an essential component of the gift of evangelist, and that is the dimension of the *visible relationships* among God's people: their love for one another, as well as their love for their neighbors. Their love was to mirror the love of God for Christ, and of Christ's love for his followers. "By this shall all men know that you are my disciples, if you have love for one another" (John 13:34).

Put all three of those dimensions together and you come up with a most helpful and enabling definition, or *algorithm*, for the gift of evangelist: (1) *proclaiming*, articulating, communicating God's good news in Christ and his New Creation; (2) visibly

---

2. This recalls an occasion at the height of the nuclear arms race, when I was persuaded by a group of scientist and others staging a public protest against nuclear arms to be the spokesperson for the Christian position against such a nightmare. I was not all comfortable being on a public platform in the city square, but was able to use it to give theological and Christian ethical reasons to oppose such (with suspicious government agents roaming crowd taking pictures). Those occasions to exercise the gift of evangelist come in odd forms and often unexpected times.

demonstrating the *lifestyle* of that New Creation so that people will recognize something remarkable (God's glory) in your life; and (3) the loving *relationships* that demonstrate the same selfless love with which Christ has loved us (even when we were his enemies), i.e., New Creation relationships.

Those three together express the gift of evangelist in its fullness, and when any one of them is neglected, the work, or gift, of the evangelist is somehow essentially incomplete . . . the three together give the gift its authenticity in our lives. It is here, also, that the very beautiful role of the *homebrew church* comes into play. It comes into play in the *one another* dynamics, and in the interanimation with others to whom we are accountable and for whom we are responsible, and when we are able to encourage and refine and equip one another for the exercise of that gift in the daily course of our lives. We are taught in the Scriptures that we are to stir one another up to love and good works (Hebrews 10:24). We are to have the word of Christ dwelling richly among us as we teach and admonish one another (Colossians 3:16), and we can share our stories of fruitfulness, failure, and frustration . . . and pray for one another specifically as we seek to be faithful in our daily rounds.

The Demeanor of the Evangelist

Right away, in defining the demeanor, or the attitude, that should pertain in our exercise of this gift comes the place of *gentleness* and of *sensitivity*.[3] When Peter wrote to the scattered colonies of Christ's followers, he acknowledged that they were *aliens and exiles*, and that the context was unfriendly, if not downright hostile. His word to them? It was that they were to live out their lives of love and good works, first of all. He reasoned that even hostile people would have a difficulty criticizing their New Creation lifestyle.

At the same time, he reminded his readers that their lifestyle might well trigger inquiry and curiosity about the reason for their hope, and hope against such odds (1 Peter 3:13–17). With

---

3. This means that we never *assault* others with gospel propositions.

that possibility in view, they needed to always be ready to give a thoughtful, or reasonable, response . . . but note: they were to do it with *gentleness* and *respect*. Yes, those inquirers are frequently suspicious of those who come to them with "truth claims," and they resist authoritarians. But, if we approach them with gentleness and respect, we are able, then, to sow the seed of the gospel, to articulate our message about the life and teaching of Jesus Christ, and we just may get a positive hearing. Our demeanor in exercising this gift is foundational.[4]

The Evangelist Is a Listener

So much of the context of the exercising of this gift is in unexpected (or "curbstone") conversations, those informal, often unexpected occasions over coffee or beer, or in offhand conversations with colleagues at work, or on campus—even with total strangers who initiate conversation. In such conversations, we don't realistically know what is going on in their lives, so it might just help to propose, "Tell me about yourself." They may respond that it's none of your business, but many, if not most, of such conversation partners harbor deep loneliness, and so in response to such a question may crack the door into their lives. They might be resistant to such a question, but at the same time intrigued that you even care. They might be downright surprised that anyone cares enough to ask.

But careful listening in conversations is the priority. As one old Texan put it, "When you're talking, you ain't learning nuthin." Our affirmation of what is commendable in their lives can possibly lead them to further openness. If we are patient, it is not unusual for such persons to, sooner or later, want to know about us. Then we have the right to give them that thoughtful answer . . . with gentleness.

---

4. One thinks of the response of a Dublin newspaper when the Irish poet Seamus Haney died. He was so loved, the paper reported, because four words described his life: *warmth, humor, caring,* and *courtesy.* Those four words might well describe the demeanor of any who would faithfully exercise the gift of *evangelist.*

Being (as we are called to be) children of the Light in the cultural darkness is just that: we live in varying degrees of intellectual darkness, moral and ethical darkness, hopelessness, those trapped in dehumanizing and ethically indifferent daily occupations, or those living empty lives without meaning. Not only so, but the Scriptures make plain that such real persons and friends are *captives* to the darkness (and to Satan the prince of darkness), that they are blind and unable to see beyond their own human boundaries. That makes our calling to exercise our gift of evangelist to be one that is *humanly* impossible, which is precisely why the Scriptures are replete with the reminder that we are to be *praying always*. That is not some pious platitude . . . rather, it acknowledges, on one hand, our calling to communicate, or evangelize, but on the other hand, that it is humanly impossible to change lives and open minds—even as that is exactly what we are called to do. We are dependent on the mystical power of the Holy Spirit in such engagements (which are an act of faith . . . and often difficult to discern). God works in and through us in ways that may be (and usually are) hidden even from us.

We learn and grow into the exercise of this gift in the *doing* of it. The gift of *evangelist* makes every day with "boots on the ground," in the midst of that day's routines and vicissitudes, to be one of anticipation. "Do the work of an evangelist" (2 Timothy 4:5). We are to be contagious demonstrations of God's love for the world, of his *New Creation* in Christ, and of the joy and freedom that comes when Christ comes and takes up habitation in our lives. . . . But there is one more piece before we conclude.

"Midwifing" Others into New Life in Christ

Along the way, as we are faithful in our calling, someone may respond and ask, "What do I do now? How do I sign on as a follower of Jesus? How do I get on board?" In answer, it is useful to go back to the two words that Jesus used in calling for a response to his message: *repent* and *believe*. Or, perhaps the parallel twin concepts that Paul gives: ". . . if you *confess* with your mouth that Jesus is

The Gift of Evangelist

Lord and *believe* in your heart that God has raised him from the dead, you will be saved" (Romans 10:9–10)—confession and belief. Those two components are a good entrance point into our response to Jesus' promise to give new life to those who come to him, i.e., that, first of all, we know the *data* concerning who Jesus is, what he taught, what he promises us, and what he requires of us, in some basic way. That, in turn, calls for us to respond to a whole new way of thinking and believing in which Jesus is the focus of our lives. Then that, in turn, calls for us to go public, to confess him before others. Jesus gave the church the simple entrance rite called *baptism*, in which the person goes public with their confession of Christ, and then receives the simple symbol of water washing, or baptism.[5]

A person becomes a follower of Jesus Christ, then, as he/she arrives at a *knowledge* of Jesus, his life and teachings, his promises and commands. When that is persuasive, then one *assents* to his claims (or knowledgeably responds to his love and invitation). That knowledge and assent, then, are consummated as one e*mbraces* Jesus Christ by faith. Full disclosure here: such a life-changing encounter may take place rather quickly and unmistakably (maybe even traumatically) . . . or it may take a long season of reflection, pondering, processing, counting the cost, dealing with agonizing doubts and misunderstanding . . . but at the end of the day it is an act of mind and will, personally and publically.

Our gift of *evangelist* is a calling to being sensitive "midwives" who usher others into new life in Christ.

We come, then, to our conclusion: that it is by being equipped into our exercise of those four gifts of the Spirit that all of God's

---

5. Different Christian traditions differ on exactly how this is done, or precisely what it means, but all concur on the fact that Jesus commanded it, and that it includes one's public identification with Christ, and the cleansing or new start that it conveys. The thousands at the Pentecost miracle were somehow baptized, but then a short time later the disciple Philip baptized the Ethiopian dignitary solo in the wilderness. Repentance and faith. Personal identification with Christ and public confession.

people become mature in their calling to Christ. It is also our conclusion that some configuration of our *homebrew church* is a most essential component of God's design in recreating the human community. It is the context in which we display God's love to real *one anothers* by being mutually accountable to one another, and responsible for one another. It is the community in which we are enabled to encourage one another, to provoke one another to love and good works, to rebuke one another (and be rebuked) in love, to pray for one another realistically and specifically. It is also the community in which we are able to have the word of Christ permeating our times together and in which we can teach and admonish one another, or equip and refine one another on the basis of the word of Christ. It is the community in which we are not strangers to one another and in which we know one another's name and face and story. It is the community in which we are mutually being created to be that *beautiful bride for the Lamb of God*, which is its ultimate goal. It is the glory of God.

Chapter 8

The Book of Revelation: Living in the Apocalypse

On my part, seeking to portray a *reconceiving* of the church for the emerging generation, to the *iGens*... turning here to the weird book of Revelation, which concludes the New Testament, would seem to be a total non sequitur, or maybe more like the author taking leave of his senses. For starts, the culture and world in which we live and that of the first century are like two different planets. Be all that as it may, it is my contention that the book of Revelation is a huge gift to the church (notwithstanding all the bizarre and cockamamie interpretations that have been imposed upon it by some well-meaning persons). Its inclusion in the New Testament is not only an act of divine inspiration, but an act of genius.

It gives to us the unveiling of human history, which is so essential to our understanding and interpretation of it all, and it comes from the risen Lord Jesus himself. During the reality of so much that is tragic, and inexplicable to us . . . this book gives us *hope*, and engenders faithfulness in the church, and its calling to be the people of God's new and everlasting Kingdom, which is inaugurated in Jesus Christ.

But I need to paint in some background.

Then and Now, Them and Us

First to them, i.e., to the first-century church: in view of my proposal of *homebrew churches*, it would be accurate to say that all the first-century churches were essentially *homebrew churches*, i.e., small enclaves of those whose hearts and minds had been taken captive by the love of God made known in Jesus. They were composed of those who affirmed that new reality in their lives publicly, even if that was to risk imprisonment, torture, and death.

And note: such professions of faith put them in total opposition to the faith of the Roman Empire, in which Caesar was the undisputed lord. For the Christian folk, then, to confess that "Jesus is Lord!" was an act of sedition, and a crime against the empire. Yet to defy the dominant social order was understood by those communities to be of the essence of their calling into God's New Creation. That countercultural profession of faith also put them into tension with the influential trade guilds (their workplaces). Such unequivocal faith in Jesus, and the dominion of God, also called forth immediate resentment by the local religions, with their local deities, which were a prominent factor in the local economy of every city, what with their temples, priests, and temple trade.

The culture was hostile, through and through, and determined to exterminate any opposition or competitors. The followers of Christ knew this, and also knew that such was the very world in rebellion that God so loved . . . and in which they were to be his witnesses by their lives of love and good works. The *homebrew churches* were not escapists, but they were sober, cautious, and realistic.

Such a context made their enclaves of Christian faith, their *homebrew churches*, critical to their survival.

Then there's us!

Two millennia have passed, in which the Christian faith has become a very dominant factor in the culture (particularly in the west) even with all the aberrations and subversions that have afflicted it along the way. It was a culture-creative force. Yet, now, in the twenty-first century in the segment of the world that has been designated as *Christendom* . . . the church's influence has so diminished that it is, for the emerging generation, something of a nonfactor. Whereas the cultural context in which the church lived was for *them* hostile . . . the opposite is now true. The culture in which the church finds itself today is immunized against the church's message. It is secular, dismissive, indifferent, even contemptuous toward any faith claim such as the Christian faith embodies.

Our culture is designated by many (if not most) as *post-Christian*. This is the existential landscape that any *reconceived* church must confront.

Suffering

Again, as crazy as it may sound, it is also essential for our landscape to retrieve from the church's forgetfulness, and to dust off, the reality of *suffering* as an expected component of our following Jesus. This is not *comfort-zone Christianity*, not *health and wealth* stuff . . . rather, the New Testament documents are replete with the sobering reality that to embrace Christ is to engage in a cosmic battle with the destructive powers of darkness . . . which also involves suffering—sharing in Christ's sufferings: "For it has been granted to you to you that for the sake of Christ you should not only believe in him but also to suffer for his sake" (Philippians 1:29). Or: ". . . but we rejoice in our sufferings, knowing that suffering produces endurance, and endurance produces character, and character produces hope . . ." (Romans 5:3–5). Or again: "Beloved, do not be surprised at the fiery trial when it comes upon you to test you, as though something strange were happening to you. But rejoice insofar as you share Christ's sufferings . . . but if you are insulted for the name of Christ, you are blessed, because Christ's Spirit of glory and of God rests upon you" (1 Peter 4:14).

That is all so totally strange to our ears in our comfortable North American calling to Christ in the twenty-first century . . . though it would not be at all strange to those in the faithful and persecuted church in such places as in North Korea and in other parts of the world, and in cultures still hostile to the Christian faith. There it would not sound strange at all. Suffering is a daily prospect. It is estimated that there were more martyrs to the Christian faith in the twentieth century than in the whole history of the church previously. Yet, in the West the church made peace with the "empire" by conforming itself to that dominant order, and so more or less ceasing to be the salt of the earth and the light of the world. The result? The culture could ignore the church with impunity, even hold it in derision.

Those rare voices that were raised against the darkness paid a price. Dietrich Bonhoeffer, a key voice in the Christian protest against Adolph Hitler, was hanged for his participation in an attempt to assassinate Hitler. It was he who wrote, "When Jesus calls a man, he bids him come and die."[1] The coopted and compromised churches of the Christendom era have little influence in the cultural context of *tomorrow's children*. The light within it has been turned into a religious version of the darkness, and so is easily ignored.

That means that our *homebrew churches* in the twenty-first-century culture are in many ways faced with a lot of unexplored territory. Yet our challenge is, in the cosmic (or eschatological) sweep of history, the same as that that of our brothers and sisters in the first century, and in the opening passage of the book of Revelation. It is as germane to us as it was to them: "Do not fear what you are about to suffer . . ." (Revelation 2:10). They faced physical torture and imprisonment. We face a culture essentially immunized against the church, so as to ignore it or hold it in disdain. Our suffering is to be dismissed before the fact with a "Who cares?"

But note: Christ *is*, in fact, building his church globally. The gates of hell are not prevailing against it ultimately. The church's growth in the world of the twenty-first century is exponential, yet so often out of sight. The church, in its faithful embodiment of the gospel, is out of control, emerging in unexpected places and in

---

1. Dietrich Bonhoeffer, *The Cost of Discipleship* (London: SCM, 1948), 44.

creative and culturally sensitive forms. So, where is all this taking us? Where are we going here? Sit tight!

The Book of Revelation

When Jesus was telling his disciples of the necessity of the forthcoming Spirit for the empowering of their mission, he told them that when the Spirit came he would not only guide them into all truth, but that he would glorify the Son of God (John 16:13–14). Yes, and this is precisely what greets us at the threshold of the book of Revelation. The author (John), first off, tells us that he was *in the Spirit* on Lord's day when the ascended Lord visited him with an epiphany, or a revelation, which not only included, ultimately, guidance into that amazing unveiling of the meaning of human history, but it also began and ended with an awesome descriptions of the glory of Christ.

But note, especially, the setting: John was enduring tribulation, which called for his patient endurance ... and he was captive at a prison colony. The Lord's day would not have been a day of rest in that colony, and yet, in the very midst of it all, came this revelation. That said, we pick up on the setting of suffering as the expected experience of God's people. Yet, it was in the midst of that suffering that there came the revelation to John of the ascended Lord, described by John as being clothed in a long white robe, with a golden sash around his chest, wiht hair white like wool and white as snow. His feet were like burnished bronze, and his voice like the roar of many waters. From his mouth came a sharp and two-edged sword, and his face was like the sun shining in full strength—the glory of the Son of God. And what was this glorified Christ doing? He was walking among the seven golden lampstands, symbolic of the totality of his churches.

John, then, is commanded to write down what he sees, and so we have the book of Revelation, written out of a Roman prison colony, in the teeth of a hostile government, and yet composed in an apocalyptic language that Christ's followers would understand—but which their enemies would not. There then follow seven letters written to the symbolic seven churches of Asia Minor, but actually, a *diagnostic* set of writings that have aided the church over the centuries in discerning where they are faithful, or where they have (as per our chapter 2) "displaced, diluted, or forgotten their founding myth." In those colorful descriptions you see the early assault on the church by the inclusion of false teachers, or pathological personalities, or adoption of error. You see a church that has simply lost its passion for, and focus on, Christ. You see a church that is preoccupied with its own successes, and on its inner life, so that Christ is left outside. The only two churches of the seven that are totally commended are those who are experiencing, and being purified by, their sufferings. What we know is that these are perennial hazards to the church in whatever form it takes.

That introductory statement to the church is then followed by the invitation of the ascended Lord from heaven: "Come up here, and I will show you what is to take place after this" (Revelation 4:1). And again, John says that he was "in the Spirit" and so was enabled to see dramatic visions in a cosmic and eternal perspective of all that was taking place, and would take place as history unfolded—again, in an *apocalyptic* portrayal of the Lamb and of his engagement with history, and in his warfare with the Beast.

There are portrayed seven seals, which contain the secrets of the age, and only the Lamb, the Lion of the tribe of Judah, is enabled to open and interpret them. It portrays the prayers of God's people as being like incense and altering the course of history. The narrative is always being interrupted with anthems of praise to the Lamb who was slain. The book is heartening, realistic, dramatic, sobering, and yet ultimately filled with hope, and with the vision of the Lamb going forth to conquer his enemies, and to consign the devil and his angels to a lake of eternal fire and destruction.

All that is written to the church in this present age for the very purpose of keeping it sober and vigilant, and focused on God's design to make all things new, and to reconcile the world to himself by the blood of the Lamb. All the while, the present scene is still one of rebellion in different forms against its Creator, as we have sought to portray in these pages.

The Book of Revelation: Living in the Apocalypse

It is in the light of these realities that the book of Revelation is a huge gift to the church—and to our *homebrew churches*. The Lord's prayer begins with, "Thy kingdom come, thy will be done" (Matthew 6:10, KJV). The apostle John wrote, "The reason that the Son of God appeared was to destroy the works of the devil" (1 John 3:8). The book of Revelation unveils all this historical drama of the warfare between the Beast (the devil) and the Lamb of God in apocalyptic language, which would not be comprehended those whose ears were not attuned to the teachings of Christ.

Apocalyptic language would have been familiar to the first-century church, as it was birthed in the Jewish community of Jerusalem and Palestine, and so had deep roots in the documents that are designated by the church as *Old Testament*, which teachings travelled with the church as it expanded into the corners of the Roman world. Significant among those documents would be the book of the prophet Daniel, which significantly employed apocalyptic language. Daniel's apocalyptic images are mirrored in the book of Revelation. Even those who sought to understand Daniel in the sixth century BCE were told that its meaning would be revealed "at the time of the end" (Daniel 12:4).

Daniel is the story of four very gifted and handsome young Jews taken captive by the Babylonian conquerors of Palestine, and deported in order to put their gifts to work in the court of the emperor. It was there that they ultimately became (by the excellence of their lives and work) a very significant and visible factor in the royal court. Yet it was there that they also steadfastly maintained their faithfulness as practicing Jews who were formed by their Jewish Torah. They did this even at the risk of their lives. That produced some very dramatic and colorful accounts of the clash between them and the other members of the royal court, who were jealous of their prominence.

That theme of faithfulness in exile obviously permeated the early church, which was outlawed by, and suffered under, the Roman Empire. Quite early on the Christian faith (and church) had already permeated Rome, and even Caesar's own household, according to the apostle Paul (who himself was a prisoner there).

It was also that period of mass slaughter of Christians in public spectacles. The growing church in Rome, then, of necessity had to find ways to exist out of sight, and they chose as some of their meeting places the catacombs deep underground beneath the city. The catacombs were the burying place that was hewed out of the stone under the city, and which are the scene of seemingly endless tunnels, so that Roman soldiers were loath to go there. The Christians hewed out large chambers in which to meet, and decorated them with colorful frescoes. Prominent among those frescoes (still there) were the scenes from Daniel of the three young Jews in the fiery furnace in retribution for their faithfulness, and yet untouched and unharmed by the fire. Also, there was the fresco of Daniel in the lion's den. The prominence of the prophet Daniel is seen quite graphically there, so his use of apocalyptic (or veiled) language was evidently familiar to that early church.

So, what have we got?

The book of Revelation is an unveiling of the realities, the meaning, the interpretation of human history as that of the warfare between the Beast (the devil) and the Lamb, and with the followers of the Lamb who were his faithful witnesses: the church. The book is rich in symbols: seven seals, seven trumpets, seven horsemen, suffering saints under the altar crying out, "How long, O Lord?" Get this: it is affirmed in this vision that God's people, the saints, overcome and destroy every obstacle "... by the blood of the Lamb, by the word of their testimony, even if it cost them their lives" (Revelation 12:11).

Some interpreters liken this unique book to the impressionist painting of *Guernica* by Pablo Picasso (which portrays a famous battle in the Spanish revolution). All the components of the battle emerge, but in an impressionist form. So with the book of Revelation and its use of apocalyptic expression: all the components are there and are wonderfully explanatory of the meaning of history ... if one has eyes to see (otherwise, it is all *jabberwocky*!).

The assault on the people of the Lamb by military, economic, political, and other agents of the Beast are all portrayed there. Then, unmistakable in its meaning, there comes onto the scene a dramatic figure on a white horse, and on his robe and on his thigh are written the words, "King of kings and Lord of lords" (Revelation 19:18). This is the Lamb. Ultimately he triumphs over the Beast, "'that old serpent the devil," and casts him into lake of fire.

Ah, but also portrayed is the whole company of the Lamb's people, called out of every nation, from all tribes, and peoples, and languages—a great multitude that no one can number (7:9). The conclusion of the book of Revelation is more than awesome. God's New Creation is consummated: "I saw a new heaven and a new earth for the first heaven and the first earth had passed away . . ." (21:1).

But it doesn't stop there. In unfolds God's intent in creation: "Behold, the dwelling place of God is with men. He will dwell with them, and they will be his people, and God himself will be with them as their God. He will wipe away all tears from their eyes, and death shall be no more neither shall there be mourning or crying nor pain anymore, for the former things have passed away . . . Behold, I am making all things new" (21:3–4). Hope!

Question: Isn't All This an Act of Faith?

The question is inescapable for us as tomorrow's children approach what we have portrayed in these pages: Isn't this all an act of faith? A quest after some illusive solution? And the honest answer comes: *Of course it is*. But, then, so is its *rejection* an act of faith. At the same time, God has made himself known historically in infinite love in Jesus—"the Word became flesh and dwelt among us" (John 1:14)—who answered for us, in himself, the question: What is the meaning of our lives and of human history? Not only so, he has given us his great hope: that "Christ shall reign until he has put all his enemies under his feet. The last enemy to be destroyed is death" (1 Corinthians 15:25–26).

That means for us, then, as we seek to bring into clearer focus all that we have been proposing, that *homebrew churches* are to be our intimate and immediate communities of meaning, of reconciled relationships (or love), of hope, of engaging the realities of a preoccupied culture, and of the love of Christ in flesh and blood relationships . . . and that often through suffering! We are a part of a vast number whom no one can number. We are the people of the Lamb who inhabit this very world that God created for his glory. We are, in Christ, the community that that glory inhabits, and walks the streets of this present world in rebellion.

We, the church, are to be the incarnation of the Light in the context of an often hostile and disdainful culture of darkness. We are called to be the glory of God, the embodiment of his love for the world, by demonstrating what his *New Humanity* is all about. It is for such that we have been called. Such is our vision of the church reconceived for the emerging generation. There is never any doubt, however, that it is Christ who is building his church.

Epilogue

This book has been about taking a fresh look at God's purpose for his church. This book has proposed that the church is the *communal dimension of God's New Creation in Christ*. This book has been about *colonies of God's New Humanity*. This book has been about the church's place in a culture of exponential change—change so uncharted that institutions and traditions very familiar to recent generations are essentially unknown to their children. This book has been written in a *liminal* culture where there is no guarantee of what tomorrow holds.

This book is written to the emerging generation who are being formed in a culture not only of exponential change, but also in an explosion of knowledge that alters their sense of what is to be expected around the next corner. But the author is also aware that the event of the iPhone and of social media, what with Facebook, etc., has not only increased access to others, but also contributed to a growing sense of loneliness, and the resulting lack of experience in the more profound and interanimating face-to-face communication. The book is, therefore, written with the hope of introducing to that audience God's gift of love in the church as the recreated and truly human community God intends it to be.

It has been my intent in this book to acknowledge that God's church in history is a vast mosaic that has existed (and does exist) in numerous forms, and in many ethnic adaptations.

This is also a book about the church's missionary confrontation with its context since its beginning. Yes, and this book does not intend to be a *blueprint* to its readers, but rather something of a *recipe* of essential ingredients mined out of the biblical documents. The author of this book is aware that he intends to creatively challenge many of the assumptions that have existed pertaining to the church as primarily those of *sacralized* institutions and hierarchical forms . . . and dominated by a class of *sacralized* persons who are designated as *clergy*.

At the same time, this book is not at all seeking to demean all those persons and institutional expressions that have sought to be faithful stewards of the message and of the mission of God in the past (of which he is one) . . . only that their dominance is on the wane, and not an acknowledged or even recognized factor with the emerging generation. The author is most thankful for the church's past . . . but not captive to it. The church has been, from its birth, and in the most distressing or culturally resistant times, expressed in small colonies, in house churches, in intimate communities, in clandestine conventicles, in intentional communities of Christ's followers, and of every description . . . in other words, *homebrew churches*, which are expressions of the *one another* love that the Spirit creates among them, and in which one can come out of hiding, and be no longer anonymous and no longer lonely, but rather become *truly human*, free, filled with hope, and "absurdly happy."[1]

What I've been working on in these pages is not a pattern so much as an encouragement, a direction in reconceiving the church in terms of relationships that nurture and form God's *New Humanity* in Christ—to give it authenticity and "street cred," to cause it to be contagious, and an inescapable factor once again in this *whitewater* period of cultural change, to be again (as D. T. Niles described it years ago) where "one beggar tells another where to find bread." Something like that.

Such is my hope as I offer this to my readers.

---

1. A quote attributed to F. R. Maltby, who described Christians as "absurdly happy, completely fearless, and constantly in trouble."

www.ingramcontent.com/pod-product-compliance
Lightning Source LLC
Chambersburg PA
CBHW070511090426
42735CB00012B/2732